# THE FLOWER GARDEN

## JOHN NEGUS

# CONTENTS

This edition published in 1989
by Octopus Books Limited,
a division of the Octopus Publishing Group,
Michelin House,
81 Fulham Road,
London SW3 6RB

Copyright © Hennerwood Publications Limited, 1986

ISBN 0 7064 3351 3

Produced by Mandarin Offset
Printed and Bound in Hong Kong

# INTRODUCTION

**M**an cannot live by potatoes alone! They might ensure the survival of the body but they do little for the spirit. No – he needs flowers to brighten his life. Keep your eye on gardens over the years and you'll see the vegetable plot grow in size as another self-sufficiency craze comes round. A few years later, when the novelty fades, the plot begins to shrink until, perhaps, it disappears altogether. Not so the flowers; they remain popular whatever the whims of society.

Everywhere in Britain, from the humblest worker's terrace cottage to the largest stately home, flowers are tucked into beds and borders. The planting may be sparse (just a few rose bushes) or elaborate (a fully fledged bedding scheme), but these bits of earth are specially prized by the gardener.

Every gardener is faced with a choice when it comes to flower gardening. Either he can take a road that offers a minimum of work as well as a good show of flowers, or he can go the whole hog and develop a seasonal pattern of planting that ensures the maximum amount of blooms in spring, summer, autumn or winter. Most gardeners do a bit of both, making 'mixed borders' in most parts of the garden, and giving over some areas to 'bedding' – those plants that are planted in one season to flower in the next before being uprooted and replaced once more.

But no two gardens are alike, and neither are any two gardeners. One man's tasteful colour scheme is another man's psychedelic nightmare. Well, almost. John Negus has allowed for that. Here he offers an amazingly comprehensive choice of plants set out so as to make their selection for your particular garden and your particular needs as easy as pie.

For a start, he shows which plants can be grown in a variety of situations. Gardeners on clay or chalk, or those with shady borders, will find this particularly useful, for all too many books assume that every plot is carved out of rich loam in a sunny, sheltered valley. If you want to put together a particular colour scheme, everything you need is here, from the plant's identity to its height and flowering season. Just a little research beforehand can make all the difference between success or failure of a planting scheme.

There are tips, too, on using colour and texture to good effect. Now it's all too easy to become airy-fairy in the subject of garden design, but a few basic rules will at least prevent your eyes from becoming bored sooner than is necessary. With all this information on what goes where, using colours and textures, and getting your timetable right, it shouldn't be long before that once tolerable strip of dark earth becomes a bright border of beautiful blooms. At least, that's the theory. All you have to do now is put it into practice!

# FLOWERS IN THEIR SETTING

An imaginative blend of well-chosen plants is the key to a successful and beautiful flower garden. The candidates are annuals and biennials, and perennials, which include herbaceous plants, bulbs and shrubs.

The garden in bloom. The picture represents a period from spring to summer, with a fine array of colour contributed by bulbs, bedding plants, perennials, shrubs and trees. Key to numbers on plan: 1 Pansy, 2 Crocus, 3 Tulip, 4 Daffodil, 5 Polyanthus, 6 Helenium, 7 Rose-of-Sharon (Hypericum), 8 Pink (Dianthus), 9 Clematis, 10 Canadian spruce (Picea), 11 Lavender, 12 Rose 'Pink Perpetue', 13 Rose 'Paul's Scarlet Climber', 14 Laburnum, 15 Hyacinth, 16 Alyssum, 17 Petunia, 18 Variegated plantain lily (Hosta), 19 Hollyhock, 20 Lobelia, 21 Antirrhinum, 22 St John's wort (Hypericum), 23 Periwinkle (Vinca), 24 Paper-bark maple (Acer), 25 Grape hyacinth (Muscari), 26 Foxglove (Digitalis), 27 Japanese azalea, 28 Variegated ivy (Hedera), 29 Deutzia, 30 Corylopsis, 31 Plantain lily (Hosta), 32 Forget-me-not (Myosotis), 33 Bergenia, 34 Japanese spurge (Pachysandra).

**Far right** *Creating a galaxy of summer colour, half-hardy annual petunias are ideal for hanging baskets, window-boxes, fringing a border or brightening a corner.*

# PLANT TYPES

### ANNUALS

These grow from seed, flower and die all within the year. Hardy annuals, such as calendula, clarkia, cornflower and larkspur are sown where they are to flower as soon as the soil is warm enough in spring. Half-hardy annuals – the majority of bedding plants, including the showy and colourful petunia, salvia, zinnia and antir-rhinum – are sown in pots or seed trays in a propagator indoors or in a greenhouse in late winter and early spring. They are hardened off for planting out when frosts finish in May and early June.

**Near right** *Charming heralds of spring, crocuses grow from corms (thickened stem bases). There are dozens of species and varieties that colour the garden from October to March.*

### PERENNIALS

These include herbaceous plants – border kinds that die back to a crown in autumn – which live for many years: achilleas, kniphofias, delphiniums and rudbeckias are examples. Other perennials are bulbs, which include favourites like tulips, daffodils, and crocuses; shrubs, such as weigela, forsythia and viburnum; and, of course, trees. But we usually exclude large trees from most average-sized gardens as their roots can endanger foundations and absorb soil moisture for many yards around them, while their spreading branches cast excessive shade. Only the smaller kinds are acceptable, such as flowering cherries, laburnum, crab apples, and some maples.

**Near right** *Like other yarrows, Achillea 'Moonshine' is a hardy border perennial valued for its flat, bright yellow flower-heads and handsome feathery, grey-green leaves. It looks especially fine with purple-leaved sage (Salvia officinalis 'Purpurascens).*

### BIENNIALS

These have two growing seasons in which to complete their life cycle. In the first year they make a sturdy rosette of leaves. In the second they flower and die. Examples are Canterbury bells, forget-me-nots, Brompton stocks and foxgloves. Wallflowers are also included in this category, although they are actually perennials. If, however, they are left to grow on from year to year they become gaunt and leggy and flower poorly.

**Far right** *There are several forms of the spring-flowering shrub Weigela florida, whose pink or reddish-pink, funnel-shaped flowers look superb when backed by golden-leaved shrubs.*

## DESIGN

Planting schemes demand boldness: there should be no skimping. Most plants should be arranged in generous groups – two or three shrubs, three to five herbaceous perennials, and eight to 12 bulbs in a group, rather than spaced out individually. The exception to this rule is very large shrubs.

When you design or re-design a garden, it helps to draw an accurate scale plan on paper first. Begin with a site plan, showing the outline of the house, the positions of the boundaries or existing fences, and any special features, such as a beautiful existing tree, that might play an important part in the ultimate plan.

When drawing the plan, work either in the metric scale of 10 mm on the plan being equivalent to 1 m in the garden (1:100), or if you prefer Imperial measurements, work on the basis of $\frac{1}{8}$ in on the scale plan representing 1 ft in the garden (1:96). Mark the direction of north on the plan. Finally, photocopy the plan three or four times.

Whatever your size and type of garden, the centre should be kept open. This does not necessarily mean that the borders on either side must be symmetrical; in fact, they will probably look more attractive if they are somewhat off-centre. Features, such as ornaments, island beds, rockeries, pools, and specimen trees that will be used as a focal point in the design should be positioned away from the house.

A number of features can be used effectively as focal points in a garden. Whatever you choose should be positioned as far away from the vantage point as is practical, so that you encompass the greatest possible area. An effective and not-too-expensive object to act as a feature is a well-shaped, colourful tree or shrub or a conifer set in an expanse of lawn.

*Plant containers come in many shapes and sizes. Even if you have plenty of space in your borders, containers will be useful for making a feature of particular plants, for creating interest at different levels, and for ringing the changes on the sites of favourite flowers.*

### CONTAINERS

The most 'instant' garden of all is the one you plant in containers. Buy a window-box (or build your own) or get a tub from your local garden centre or shop, add a bag of compost and a tray of bedding plants in flower and in a very short time you have colour right on your window sill.

Containers are made in several different kinds of material and it is important to choose the material that suits both you and your garden. Plastic saves the most labour and it is usually cheapest, too. It is lightweight, colour-fast, and, unless it gets cracked or torn, will last for a long time, although it is liable to become brittle after several years in the sunlight.

There is a host of other containers to choose from. Terracotta pots look and feel good; wooden tubs are handsome but should be protected against rots; old wooden wheelbarrows have distinctive charm and look quaint if piled with geraniums, fuchsias and petunias; ancient kitchen coppers and canteen-sized kettles also make good plant-holders. Make sure they all have drainage holes.

Window-boxes are most successful and safest if they are designed for the space in question; when filled with plants and soil they can be extremely heavy, so they need to be very stable.

Containers make perfect homes for spring and summer bedding plants, dwarf conifers, heathers, orange and lemon trees, small rhododendrons and azaleas, and rock plants.

# LOCATION

Assessing the site is one of the first things to do when planning a garden. All plots are different; even if they are the same size and in the same road, the conditions found in each will demand differing approaches. One plot may be bathed in sun while, next door, a tall tree may plunge part of that garden into deep shadow. Winds may make it necessary to install a windbreak in one garden, while in another breezes may he hardly noticeable. Each plot must be judged on its own characteristics.

## SITE & SOIL

The type of vegetation already growing in a plot is often a good indicator of the nature of the soil. If gardens are lush with rhododendrons and azaleas in the spring and there is an abundance of heathers throughout the year, it is certain that the soil is acid. On the other hand, if the surrounding countryside is supporting luxurious growths of traveller's joy (old man's beard), whose botanical name is *Clematis vitalba*, the soil is definitely chalky. The point to bear in mind is that some plants are lime-haters while others cannot thrive in acid soils. If you are starting a garden from scratch it's a good idea to buy an inexpensive soil-testing kit. Test the soil in several places all over the garden: it is possible that it will prove to be acid in one spot and alkaline at a point only a few yards away. Mark your results on your site plan.

pool as a special feature. Indicate any such wet areas on the site plan.

It is also important to mark the position of any places where the soil appears to be exceptionally dry, so that planting can be carried out accordingly.

*Right Clematis grow naturally on chalky (limy) soil. But lime is not essential for success with garden hybrids, such as this* Clematis *'Ville de Lyon', which flowers from July to October.*

**Above** *Heather or ling* (Calluna vulgaris) *enriches many of our upland moors with a cloak of purple in early autumn, thriving on acid soil. Garden forms have buttercup-yellow and coppery red leaves that colour borders in winter.*

Sometimes a barren site will have a small area where water collects, so that the soil remains permanently wet or water-logged. If this spot is covered in vegetation it may not be easy to detect; but a preponderance of marsh plants – rushes, reeds and sedges – among the wild flora will give a good indication of such a problem. If the whole plot shows signs of being wet, the ground will need to be drained. Such a spot in only one part of the site, however, provides the opportunity to have a marsh garden or natural

## ASPECT

How the site is positioned in relation to the points of compass is the next consideration. The aspect bears on the 'well-being' of a garden in two main ways. First, it determines how much sun the garden enjoys and at what time of the day certain parts of the area are in sun or shade. Second, the aspect of a plot will in some cases – coastal districts and very exposed inland areas in particular – determine what spots in the garden are exposed to strong winds and so need to be screened.

The best aspect for a rear garden in the northern hemisphere is south or, better still, south-west. It will get the maximum amount of sun during the day: if the garden is not over-shadowed, the sun will shine on it from early or mid-morning until evening. The principal draw-back to such an aspect is that in some districts it may be exposed to strong south-westerly winds, although these are usually relatively warm.

The worst aspects for a garden are east and north. In the case of the latter, the amount of sun that shines directly on the garden may be restricted, while a garden that faces east is likely to be in shade during the afternoon. In addition, the winds that blow from north and east are often strong and biting, and if the site is in a very open position, such as on the outskirts of a town, this could have a damaging effect on plants. West and north-west are much more favourable aspects as they provide a certain amount of warmth, shade and moisture.

**Above** *Perfect for planting in gaps in crazy paving or on rock garden screes in full sun, stonecrop (Sedum) quickly forms a weed-proof carpet and flowers profusely in summer. This version is S. lydium.*

**Left** *Skimmia* japonica *is a handsome evergreen shrub that thrives in partial shade. Its glossy leaves and brilliant berries bring autumn and winter colour to the garden.*

## KNOW YOUR SOIL

Soil has to be improved, modified or manipulated so that the best conditions for plant life can be created. Good soils offer anchorage and support, sufficient food, warmth, moisture and oxygen, and room for plants to develop.

The critical soil factors for effective gardening are: land drainage, moisture retention, food content, acidity or chalkiness, and temperature. Fertile soil is easily worked and crumbly. It is dark in colour, well-drained and yet retains moisture for growth. It contains reserves of plant food to support sturdy, balanced plant growth. Examination of good soil will show moist crumbs of solid matter, pieces of old root-fibre, small pebbles, a worm or two – and innumerable tiny life-forms.

### SOIL TESTING

A trial dig to a spade's depth or more will reveal much about a piece of ground. Under wet conditions, clay soils will have puddles on the surface, and be greasy to the touch, and will stick tenaciously to your spade. A sandy soil will be well drained and gritty; feet and spade are easily cleaned, and the hole dug with comparative ease. Loams lie between the two extremes.

Under dry summer conditions clay soils become cracked, hard to cultivate, and lumpy. Conversely, sandy soil is easy to dig and is dry and dusty.

Digging chalk soils will reveal the tell-tale whitish subsoil of chalk or limestone, and whitish coloured lumps in the soil. Peat soils are usually dark, spongy and fibrous.

### WHAT'S YOUR GARDEN MADE OF?

| SOIL | APPEARANCE | PHYSICAL QUALITIES | CHEMICAL STATUS |
|------|-----------|--------------------|-----------------|
| CLAY | Soil lies under water in wet weather. Sedges, rushes, buttercup, alder, willow in evidence. | Very slow to drain. Adhesive, greasy if wet or hard and lumpy when dry. | Naturally rich in plant food. |
| HEAVY LOAM | Intermediate between clay and medium loam | | |
| MEDIUM LOAM | Strong-growing roses, shrubs and grasses. | Drains moderately quickly. Worked fairly readily. | Usually well supplied with plant food. |
| LIGHT LOAM | Intermediate between medium and sandy soil. | | |
| SANDY | Light coloured soil. Gorse, broom and Scots pine, heather and rhododendrons. | Quick draining. Easily worked in most conditions. Gritty to the touch. | Low in nutrients. Often very acid. Needs regular feeding. |
| CHALK OR LIMESTONE | White or whitish subsoil. Dogwood, viburnum and clematis flourish. | Chalk is pasty when moist. Limestone is gritty to the touch. | Low in organic matter. Alkaline. |
| PEATY | Dark fibrous soil. Alder and willow trees often present. | Spongy and fibrous. | Low in phosphates. Usually acid. |
| STONY | Often light-coloured. Many stones on surface. Sparse vegetation. Mountain ash present. | Shallow soils with large proportion of rock and stone. | Low nutrient content. Needs regular and heavy feeding. |

*It's important to know whether your soil is acid, alkaline or neutral. You can easily find out by using a soil-testing kit (left), which depends on the colour a chemical solution turns when mixed with a soil sample. The electronic meter (right) indicates the soil's pH (relative acidity or alkalinity) on a dial.*

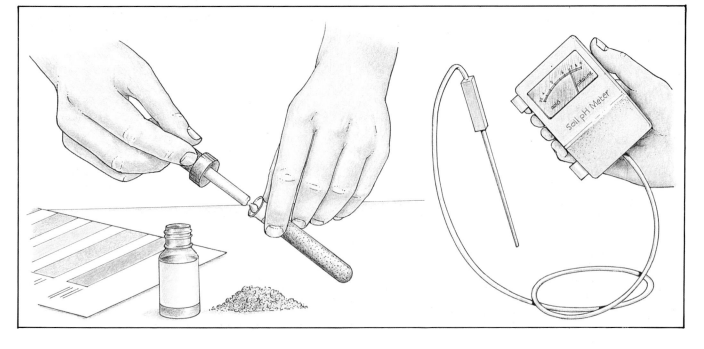

## DRAINAGE

When making a new garden or improving an established site, check the drainage by making a test dig. During the winter, dig out a hole 600 mm (2 ft) deep and cover it to prevent rain falling in. Inspect the hole daily, replacing the cover each time. If after 48 hours following heavy rain, less than 450 mm (18 in) of soil shows above the water table or water level, then attention to drainage is needed, especially if trees are to be planted. Surplus moisture in gardens is best drained by means of a soakaway or underground pipes or channels.

## ENRICHING THE SOIL

There are two groups of manure: those which breakdown readily to release plant food; and those, such as peat, which are much slower to decompose, providing little by way of plant nutrients, but, like the former, improve the soil's humus content. The first group includes farmyard manure, composted straw or garden waste material, spent mushroom compost, and seaweed. Peat, pulverized tree bark, leaf mould, and spent hops belong in the second group.

## FERTILIZERS

Some fertilizers are used as a base dressing *before* planting; others are applied as a top dressing while plants are growing. Base and top dressings usually provide the main needs of nitrogen, phosphate and potash.

Base fertilizers are mostly available as ordinary or high-potash types. The ordinary grades contain equal proportions of nitrogen, phosphate and potash, and are used for general feeding. The high-potash types are designed for

fruit and flower crops and contain twice the amount of potash.

Top dressings are applied dry or as a liquid feed. Proprietary brands are sold as three grades: *high nitrogen*, used for celery and cucumbers; *ordinary grade*, for bringing on young plants; and *high potash*, for fruit and flowers.

### PROPRIETARY FERTILISERS

| MATERIAL | INGREDIENTS (%) | | | TYPE |
|---|---|---|---|---|
| | N | P | K | |
| Bonemeal | 4 | 21 | — | Base |
| Hoof-and-horn | 13–14 | — | — | Base |
| Potassium nitrate | 15 | — | 45 | Top |
| Nitro-chalk | 15.5 | — | — | Top |
| Sulphate of ammonia | 21 | — | — | Base and top |
| Sulphate of potash | — | — | 48–50 | Base and top |
| Super-phosphate | — | 16–18 | — | Base and top |

*N = nitrogen, P = phosphorous, K = potassium*

# WHAT GROWS WHERE

Situation and aspect govern plant selection; so to a lesser extent does soil type. Fortunately, most plants are very adaptable: although they may prefer a particular kind of soil, they will usually tolerate most reasonably fertile ones that are neither too wet nor too dry for long periods. Most fussy are the lime haters, such as enkianthus, gentians, lithospermum, rhododendrons and azaleas, and most heathers (with the exception of some ericas).

Your garden's situation affects its exposure to wind and temperature, factors which influence growth. There are hillside and seaside gardens in which it is almost impossible to develop a planting scheme until winds have been softened by shelter belts of evergreen trees and shrubs and carefully sited filter-fences.

Before you buy any plants, look in neighbours' gardens and note what grows well. Talk to local experts and attend gardening-club meetings to glean all you can about the kind of plants that thrive in your district.

### PLANTS FOR ACID SOIL

Lime-hating plants thrive on acid, peaty loam soils. Some, such as camellias, rhododendrons and azaleas, also enjoy dappled shade and need shelter for spring frosts which can blacken their blooms. If you are trying to grow acid-soil lovers on ground which contains a trace of lime, water the foliage with sequestered-iron solution.

*Many garden plants are lime-haters and do best in acid soils. Typical of these are the rhododendrons and azaleas, of which this example is R. 'King George'. Such plants can sometimes be persuaded to grow in marginally chaky soil if it is given an annual dose of sequestered iron, a spring feed of seaweed fertilizer, and a generous mulch of peat or forest bark.*

*Clove-scented pinks (Dianthus) love a sunny bank to sprawl upon. Easily propagated by pegging down shoots, which root where they press against the soil, pinks flower for most of the summer. This one is the modern garden variety 'Show Celebrity'.*

| PLANT | IN FLOWER | COLOURS |
|---|---|---|
| Calluna (S) | Summer, autumn | Pink, purple, red, white |
| Camellia (S) | Spring | Pink, purple, red, white |
| Clethra (S) | Summer | White |
| Daboecia (S) | Autumn | Pink, red, white |
| Enkianthus (S) | Spring | Bronze |
| Erica (most) (S) | Winter, spring, summer | Mauve, pink, red, white |
| Eucryphia (S) | Summer | White |
| Fothergilla (S) | — | Autumn foliage colours |
| Gaultheria (S) | — | Purple or red autumn fruits |
| *Gentiana sino-ornata* (R) | Autumn | Blue |
| Hamamelis (S) | Winter | Orange, red, yellow |
| Kalmia (S) | Spring, summer | Pink |
| *Lithospermum diffusum* (R) | Summer | Blue |
| Magnolia (S) | Spring | White |
| Rhododendron (S) | Spring, summer | Various |

**(H) = *Herbaceous*, (R) = *Rock plant*, (S) = *Shrub***

### PLANTS FOR CHALKY SOIL
Many plants that are reputedly lime-haters will grow in alkaline (chalky) soil if the fertile topsoil is reasonably deep. The following will do well if the soil has been well dug and enriched.

| PLANT | IN FLOWER | COLOURS |
|---|---|---|
| Agapanthus (H) | Summer | Blue, violet, white |
| Aster (A), (H) | Summer, autumn | Many |
| Aubrieta (R) | Spring | Blue, pink, purple |
| Campanula (H) | Summer | Blue, pink, purple, white |
| Cheiranthus (Bi) | Spring, summer | Orange, pink, red, yellow |
| Clematis (C) | Spring, summer, autumn | Many |
| Daphne (S) | Winter, spring | Pink, red, purple |
| Deutzia (S) | Summer | Pink, white |
| Dianthus (H) | Summer | Many |
| Eranthis (B) | Winter, spring | Yellow |
| Erica (some) (S) | Autumn, winter | Various |
| Hebe (S) | Summer, autumn | Pink, purple, white |
| Hypericum (S) | Summer | Yellow |
| Papaver (A), (H) | Summer | Various |
| Saxifraga (R) | Spring, summer, autumn | Various |
| Syringa (H) | Spring, summer | Pink, purple, white |

| | | |
|---|---|---|
| **(A) = *Annual*** | **(C) = *Climber*** | **(S) = *Shrub*** |
| **(B) = *Bulb*** | **(H) = *Herbaceous*** | |
| **(Bi) = *Biennial*** | **(R) = *Rock plant*** | |

### PLANTS FOR SUNNY PLACES
Most plants enjoy an open, sunny position and the majority that compose the framework of the flower garden will benefit from maximum light at all times. The following are very colourful kinds that cheer us through spring and summer. They are also tolerant of partial shade: they will thrive if they receive direct sunlight for only half the day, provided there is strong indirect light for the other half.

| PLANT | IN FLOWER | COLOURS |
|---|---|---|
| Achillea (H) | Summer | Yellow |
| Agapanthus (H) | Summer | Blue, white |
| *Alstroemeria ligtu* (H) | Summer | Orange, pink, white |
| Centaurea (H) | Summer | Blue, pink, purple, red, white |
| Cistus (S) | Summer | Pink, red, white |
| Choisya (S) | Spring, autumn | White |
| Cytisus (S) | Spring | Pink, purple, white, yellow |
| Dianthus (H) | Summer | Pink, red, white |
| Eryngium (H) | Summer | Blue, white |
| Escallonia (S) | Summer | Pink, red, white |
| Genista (S) | Spring, summer | Yellow |
| Geranium (H) | Summer | Blue, pink, red |
| Helianthemum (S) | Summer | Pink, red, white, yellow |
| Hemerocallis (H) | Summer | Bronze, yellow |
| *Iris germanica* (H) | Spring | Various |
| Kniphofia (H) | Summer | Orange, red, yellow |
| Lavandula (S) | Summer | Blue, purple |

| PLANT | IN FLOWER | COLOURS |
|---|---|---|
| *Linum perenne* (H) | Summer | Blue |
| Oenothera (H) | Summer | Yellow |
| Rosmarinus (S) | Spring | Blue |
| Spartium (S) | Summer | Yellow |
| Santolina (S) | Summer | Yellow |
| Verbascum (H) | Summer | Biscuit, pink, yellow |

*(H) = Herbaceous; (S) = Shrub*

## PLANTS FOR SHADE

All plants need light to survive, but not all of them need brilliant sunshine. Natives of woodland, in particular, are happiest when given some protection from the sun's rays. All the plants listed below will tolerate shade to a greater or lesser degree. If the soil is too dry – that, for instance, under a large tree usually is – improve its moisture-retaining properties by digging in plenty of organic manure. Rhododendrons, azaleas, camellias and hydrangeas are a few of many superb plants that thrive in little sunshine. If the right plants are chosen, there is no reason why shady spots should be dull places. Many foliage plants grow well in shade, including ferns, of which there are many fully hardy and highly ornamental kinds.

| PLANT | IN FLOWER | COLOURS |
|---|---|---|
| Acanthus (H) | Summer | Purple, white |
| Aconitum (H) | Summer | Blue |
| Ajuga (H) | Spring, summer | Blue |
| Alchemilla (H) | Summer | Yellow |
| *Allium moly* (B) | Summer | Yellow |
| *Anemone blanda* (B) | Spring | Blue |
| Aruncus (H) | Summer | White |
| *Asperula odorata* (H) | Spring | White |
| Astilbe (H) | Summer | Pink, red white |
| Astrantia (H) | Summer | Pink, white |
| Bergenia (H) | Spring | Pink, red |
| Brunnera (H) | Spring | Blue |
| Camassia (B) | Summer | Blue |
| Camellia (S) | Spring | Various |
| Convallaria (H) | Spring | White |
| Corydalis (H) | Spring, summer | Yellow |
| Cyclamen (B) | Spring, summer | Pink |
| *Daphne mezereum* (S) | Winter, spring | Red, violet, white |
| Dicentra (H) | Spring | Pink |
| Digitalis (Bi) | Summer | Rose-pink |
| Endymion (B) | Spring | Blue |
| Epimedium (H) | Spring | Pink, yellow |
| Erythronium (B) | Spring | Mauve |
| Euonymus (S) | — | Foliage only |
| *Euphorbia robbiae* (H) | Spring | Green |
| Gaultheria (S) | — | Foliage, berries |

| PLANT | IN FLOWER | COLOURS |
|---|---|---|
| Geranium endressii (H) | Summer | Pink |
| Helleborus (H) | Spring | Green, plum |
| Hosta (H) | Summer | Mauve, white |
| *Hypericum calycinum* | Summer | Yellow |
| Liriope (H) | Autumn | Purple |
| *Lysimachia clethroides* (H) | Summer | White |
| Mahonia (S) | Winter, spring | Yellow |
| Meconopsis (H) | Summer | Blue |
| *Ornithogalum nutans* (B) | Spring | White |
| Pernettya (S) | — | Red berries |
| Polygonatum (H) | Spring | White |
| Polygonum (some) (H) | Summer | Cream, pink, red |
| Primula (some) (H) | Spring | Pink, yellow |
| Prunella (H) | Spring, summer | Blue, pink |
| Pulmonaria (H) | Spring | Blue, pink, red |
| Sanguinaria (H) | Spring | White |
| Sarcococca (S) | Winter | White |
| Skimmia (S) | Summer | White; red berries |
| Symphoricarpos (S) | — | White or pink fruits |
| Symphytum (H) | Spring | Blue, yellow |
| *Thalictrum dipterocarpum* (H) | Summer | Lilac, yellow |
| Tiarella (H) | Spring, summer | White |
| Trillium (H) | Spring | White |

*Flowering from February to April, when it brightens a shady corner under trees or in the lea of a building, the windflower (Anemone blanda 'Atrocaerulea') grows happily in deep, leafy soil.*

| PLANT | IN FLOWER | COLOURS |
|---|---|---|
| Trollius (H) | Spring | Orange, yellow |
| Viburnum (S) | Spring | White; blue or red berries |
| Vinca (H) | Spring | Blue, purple, white |
| Viola (H), (A) | Spring, summer | Various |

| | | |
|---|---|---|
| **(A) = Annual** | **(H) = Herbaceous** | |
| **(B) = Bulb** | **(S) = Shrub** | **(Bi) = Biennial** |

### PLANTS FOR DRY SOIL

Light and sandy soils have many advantages: they are easy to cultivate, they warm up quickly in spring, and they drain well after wet weather.

If sandy soil is all you have, and you want to grow plants that enjoy a modicum of moisture at the roots, there is only one thing for it: you must enrich your earth with plenty of organic matter – peat, compost, manure, leaf-mould and the like.

The plants in this list can usually tolerate dry conditions, but they will all need a helping hand in their youth. It is no good pushing their roots into dust and expecting them to survive. During the first year of establishment they will need to be soaked in dry spells so that the root system they develop is far-reaching and capable of searching for moisture. Organic matter is useful for these plants, too. And remember that when water is able to pass quickly through a soil, it often takes nutrients with it. Sandy soils are hungry soils: feed them regularly.

| PLANT | IN FLOWER | COLOURS |
|---|---|---|
| Acanthus (H) | Summer | Purple, white |
| Achillea (H) | Summer | Pink, yellow |
| Ageratum (A) | Summer | Blue, mauve, white |

| PLANT | IN FLOWER | COLOURS |
|---|---|---|
| Agrostemma (A) | Summer | Pink |
| Alchemilla (H) | Summer | Yellow |
| Anthemis (H) | Summer, autumn | White, yellow |
| Artemisia (H) | — | Silver leaves |
| Astrantia (H) | Summer | Pink, white |
| Aubrieta (R) | Spring | Mauve, pink, purple, red |
| Berberis (S) | Spring | Orange, yellow; red berries |
| Bergenia (some) (H) | Spring | Pink, red, white |
| Borago (A) | Summer | Blue |
| Buddleia (S) | Summer | Blue, mauve, red, white |
| Calluna (S) | Summer | Pink, purple, red, white |
| Campanula (Bi), (H) | Summer | Blue, violet, white |
| Cistus (S) | Summer | Pink, red, white, yellow |
| Clarkia (A) | Summer | Pink |
| Corydalis (R) | Spring, summer | Blue, yellow |
| Cosmea (A) | Summer | Orange, scarlet, yellow |
| Cotoneaster (S) | Summer | White; red berries |
| Crocosmia (H) | Summer | Orange, scarlet, yellow |
| Cytisus (S) | Spring | Cream, pink, red, yellow |
| Dierama (H) | Summer | Pink, purple, white |
| Digitalis (Bi) | Summer | Various |
| Echinops (H) | Summer | Blue |
| Echium (A) | Summer | Blue |
| Erigeron (H) | Summer | Blue, orange, pink |
| Eryngium (H) | Summer | Blue |
| Eschscholzia (A) | Summer | Orange, red, yellow |
| Gazania (A) | Summer | Yellow |
| Genista (S) | Summer | Yellow |
| Geranium (H) | Summer | Blue, pink, purple, white |
| Godetia (A) | Summer | Orange, salmon |
| Gypsophila (A), (H) | Summer | White |
| Hebe (S) | Summer | Blue, purple, red, white |
| Helianthemum (S) | Spring, summer | Pink, red, white, yellow |
| Helichrysum (A) | Summer | Orange, pink, red |
| Hibiscus (S) | Summer, autumn | Blue, mauve, red, white |
| Hypericum (S) | Summer | Yellow |
| Kniphofia (H) | Summer | Orange, red, yellow |
| Lathyrus (C) | Summer | Pink, red, white |
| Lavandula (S) | Summer | Blue, purple |
| Lavatera (S) | Summer, autumn | Pink, purple, white |

*Revelling in poor, well-drained, even dry soil in full sun, broom (this one is* Genista lydia*) unfolds its wealth of blossom in May and June. It looks particularly lovely when cascading over a low wall or rock-garden outcrop.*

| PLANT | IN FLOWER | COLOURS |
|---|---|---|
| Liatris (H) | Summer | Purple |
| Limnanthes (A) | Summer | White, yellow |
| Linaria (A), (H) | Summer | Pink, violet |
| Linum (A), (H) | Summer | Blue |
| Lychnis (H) | Summer | Pink, red |
| Macleaya (H) | Summer | Cream, white |
| Myrtus (S) | Summer | White |
| Nepeta (H) | Summer | Blue |
| Nigella (A) | Summer | Blue, pink, red, white |
| Oenothera (H) | Summer | Yellow |
| Olearia (S) | Summer | White |
| Osmanthus (S) | Spring, summer | White |
| Physalis (H) | Summer | White; red seed pods |
| Santolina (S) | Summer | Yellow; silvery leaves |
| Sarcococca (S) | Winter | White |
| Sedum (H) | Summer | Pink, red |
| Sempervivum (R) | Summer | Pink, red, yellow |
| Solidago (H) | Summer, autumn | Yellow |
| Stachys (H) | Summer | Pink, purple; silvery leaves |
| Tagetes (A) | Summer, autumn | Bronze, orange, yellow |
| Tamarix (S) | Summer | Pink |
| Vinca (H) | Spring | Blue, red, violet, white |
| Yucca (S) | Summer | White |

**(A) = Annual**     **(H) = Herbaceous**
**(Bi) = Biennial**   **(R) = Rock plant**
**(C) = Climber**     **(S) = Shrub**

## PLANTS FOR MOISTURE-RETENTIVE OR CLAY SOIL

There's no denying that clay soil is the most unpleasant kind to work, and the most back-breaking, too. But once plants are established within it they often do well, sinking their roots into a medium which seldom dries out at depth and so offers sustenance in dry summers, when plants on lighter soils are suffering.

Dig heavy soils in autumn so that the winter frosts can help shatter the clods and break them into more workable crumbs, and add as much organic matter and sharp grit as you can. Planting on soils like these is nearly always best carried out in spring.

| PLANT | IN FLOWER | COLOURS |
|---|---|---|
| Ajuga (H) | Spring, summer | Blue |
| Alchemilla (H) | Summer | Yellow |
| Astilbe (H) | Summer | Pink, red, white |
| Astrantia (H) | Summer | Pink, white |
| Brunnera (H) | Spring | Blue |
| Cimicifuga (H) | Summer | White |
| Dicentra (H) | Spring | Pink, white |

| PLANT | IN FLOWER | COLOURS |
|---|---|---|
| Dodecatheon (H) | Spring | Lilac, yellow |
| *Fritillaria meleagris* (B) | Spring | Purplish-green |
| Hemerocallis (H) | Summer | Bronze, yellow |
| Heuchera (H) | Summer | Pink, red |
| Hosta (H) | Summer | Blue, mauve, white |
| Iris (many) (H), (B) | Spring | Various |
| Lamium (H) | — | Foliage: silver, gold variegation |
| *Leucojum aestivum* (B) | Summer | White |
| *Leucojum vernum* (B) | Spring | White |
| Liriope (H) | Autumn | Purple, violet |
| Ligularia (H) | Summer | Yellow |
| Lysimachia (H) | Summer | White, yellow |
| Lythrum (H) | Summer | Pink |
| Mimulus (H) | Summer | Yellow |
| Monarda (H) | Summer | Lavender, pink, red |
| Myosotis (Bi) | Spring | Blue, pink, white |
| *Narcissus cyclamineus* (B) | Spring | Yellow |
| *Ornithogalum nutans* (B) | Spring | White |
| Polygonatum (H) | Spring | White |
| Polygonum (H) | Summer | Cream, pink, red |
| Primula (many) (H) | Spring | Various |
| Pulmonaria (H) | Spring | Blue, red; variegated foliage |
| Ruscus (S) | — | Red berries |
| Sidalcea (H) | Summer | Pink |
| Symphytum (H) | Spring | Blue, yellow |
| Thalictrum (H) | Summer | Lavender, purple, white, yellow |
| Trollius (H) | Spring | Orange, yellow |

**(B) = Bulb**       **(R) = Rock plant**
**(Bi) = Biennial**   **(S) = Shrub**
**(H) = Herbaceous**

*Prized by flower arrangers for its sprays of sulphur-yellow summer flowers, and by gardeners for the way its leaf hairs cause droplets of dew to gather like balls of quicksilver, lady's mantle (Alchemilla mollis) is a firm favourite on clay soils.*

*There are few more heartening sights on a chilly late-October day than the icing-sugar-pink flowers of the Guernsey lily (Nerine bowdenii). Colonising happily in a south- or south-west-facing border where summer sun has warmed the bulbs, it comes into flower in autumn.*

### TENDER PLANTS FOR WARM, SHELTERED POSITIONS

A good selection of frost-tender plants from warm countries will thrive in sheltered southern and western regions of the British Isles if we site them carefully. Their big enemy is wind frost, the killer that shrivels leaves and bites deep into the soil. The answer is to shield such exotics as bottle-brush (*Callistemon*) and lobster's claw (*Clianthus*) by setting them at the foot of a south or west facing wall, or in some sun-drenched corner.

| PLANT | IN FLOWER | COLOURS |
|---|---|---|
| Agapanthus (H) | Summer | Blue, violet-purple, white |
| *Amaryllis belladonna* (B) | Summer, autumn | Pink |
| *Ballota pseudodictamnus* (H) | Summer, autumn | Foliage: woolly white leaves |
| Berberidopsis (C) | Late summer | Crimson, yellow |
| *Buddleia fallowiana* (S) | Summer | Lavender |
| Callistemon (S) | Summer | Red |
| *Camellia sasanqua* (S) | Spring | Pink, red, white |
| Campsis (C) | Summer, autumn | Orange |
| *Centaurea gymnocarpa* (H) | — | Foliage: silvery leaves |
| *Chrysanthemum ptarmacaefolium* (H) | — | Foliage: lacy white leaves |
| Clerodendron (S) | Summer, autumn | Red |
| Clianthus (C) | Spring, summer | Red |
| Crinum (B) | Summer, autumn | Pink |
| *Convolvulus cneorum* (S) | Summer | White |
| *Dimorphotheca ecklanis* (H) | Summer | Purple, white |
| Eccremocarpus (C) | Summer | Orange, red |
| Gazania (H) | Summer | Brown, orange, red, pink, yellow |
| Hebe hybrids (S) | Summer | Pink, purple, red, white |
| *Helichrysum petiolatum* (H) | — | Foliage: grey-green leaves |
| *Indigofera potaninii* (S) | Summer, autumn | Pink |
| *Jasminum officinalis* (S) | Summer | White |
| Lampranthus (Mesembryanthemum) (S) | Summer | Red |
| *Mutisia clematis* (S) | Summer | Orange-pink |
| Nerine (B) | Autumn | Pink, red, white |
| *Olearia semidentata* (S) | Summer | Purple |
| *Passiflora caerulea* (C) | Summer | Blue/white |
| Piptanthus (S) | Spring | Yellow |
| *Teucrium fruticans* (S) | Summer | Blue |
| Tigridia (B) | Summer | Red, white, yellow |
| Trachelospermum (C) | Summer | White |
| *Tropaeolum tuberosum* (C) | Summer, autumn | Red, yellow |

| | |
|---|---|
| **(B) = Bulb** | **(H) = Herbaceous** |
| **(C) = Climber** | **(S) = Shrub** |

## PLANTS FOR GROUND COVER

Gardeners have been planting things closely together for hundreds of years, both for the mat-like effect of growth as well as to keep down weeds. Today the idea has caught on as a labour-saving device.

The earth must be well cultivated, weeded and fertilised and the plants given every encouragement to grow well from the outset. This means that they will have to be thoroughly watered in dry spells, and that they will have to be weeded among until their leaves meet to form an impenetrable rug of growth.

When it comes to calculating how many plants you will need, bear in mind the ultimate spread of the species chosen. Plant so that the individuals will overlap slightly when they have been growing for a season or two.

| PLANT | IN FLOWER | COLOURS |
|---|---|---|
| Acaena (R) | — | Metallic blue leaves |
| Ajuga (H) | Spring, summer | Purple |
| Alchemilla (H) | Summer | Yellow-green |
| Arundinaria (dwarf species) (S) | — | Feathery bamboo |
| Bergenia (H) | Spring | Pink, red, white |
| Brunnera (H) | Spring | Blue |
| Calamintha (H) | Summer | Lavender |
| Calluna (S) | Summer, autumn | Mauve, pink, purple, white |
| Cistus (S) | Summer | Pink, red, white, yellow |
| Convallaria (H) | Spring | White |
| *Cornus canadensis* (H) | Summer | White |
| *Cotoneaster* 'Skogsholm' | — | Red berries |
| Epimedium (H) | Spring | Pink, red, yellow |
| Erica (S) | Winter, spring, summer | Mauve, pink, red, white |
| *Euonymus fortunei* (S) | — | Variegated foliage |
| Euphorbia (some) (H) | Spring, summer | Yellow |
| Gaultheria (S) | — | Purple or red autumn fruits |
| Hebe (S) | Summer | Blue, purple, red, white |
| Hedera (S) | — | Varied foliage |
| Helianthemum (S) | Spring, summer | Pink, red, white, yellow |
| Hosta (H) | Summer | Blue, mauve, white; decorative leaves |
| Hypericum (S) | Summer | Yellow |
| Iberis (A) | Spring | White |
| Juniperus (some) (S) | — | Foliage: blue, green, grey or yellow |
| Lamium (H) | — | Foliage: varieties in gold, silver |

| PLANT | IN FLOWER | COLOURS |
|---|---|---|
| Lavandula (S) | Summer | Blue, purple |
| Liriope (H) | Autumn | Purple, violet |
| *Lysimachia nummularia* (H) | Summer | Yellow |
| *Mahonia aquifolium* | — | Black berries |
| Nepeta (H) | Summer | Blue |
| *Pachysandra terminalis* (S) | — | Foliage: pale green or variegated |
| Pernettya (S) | — | Pink, red or white berries |
| Potentilla (H), (S) | Summer | White, yellow |
| Pulmonaria (H) | Spring | Blue, red; variegated foliage |
| Ruscus (S) | — | Red berries |
| Santolina (S) | Summer | Yellow; silvery foliage |
| Sarcococca (S) | Winter | White |
| Skimmia (S) | Summer | White; red berries |
| Stachys (H) | Summer | Pink, purple; silvery leaves |
| Symphytum (H) | Spring, summer | Red, yellow |
| Thymus (R) | Summer | Lilac |
| Tiarella (H) | Spring | White |
| Vaccineum (S) | Spring | Pink |
| Vinca (H) | Spring | Blue, red, violet, white |
| Viola (A), (H) | Spring, summer | Various |

| (A) = Annual | (R) = Rock plant |
|---|---|
| (H) = Herbaceous | (S) = Shrub |

*Valued for its exquisitely marbled leaves, which even in winter remain dry and leathery, barrenwort (Epimedium) forms a carpet of foliage no weed can penetrate. There are species with white, yellow, red and orange columbine-like flowers in late spring. This one is E. perralderianum.*

## PLANTS FOR SEASIDE GARDENS

Coastal gardens have the great advantage of a fairly stable climate, thanks to the presence of the sea, whose temperature fluctuates very slowly. Such gardens, however, are apt to suffer at the hands of the wind, which lashes them with salt spray in autumn and winter.

Some plants can cope with this kind of treatment, and even though many of them look badly burned after a severe gale, they will soon produce new leaves when favourable weather returns.

Gardens right on the sea front are the most difficult to plant, and it is essential that some form of windbreak is provided before planting gets underway. Wattle hurdles and other semi-permeable barriers should be erected before salt-tolerant hedges, such as tamarisk and juniper, are established to make a more durable shield.

That done, the gardener can experiment with a varied group of plants, even though his season may be shorter than that of gardens inland. The first gales of autumn are always awaited with dread!

*Provided you shield it from the direct onslaught of a salty wind, the Peruvian lily (Alstroemeria aurantiaca) will colour a border in summer with a multiplicity of fiery orange blooms. It spreads by underground stems, and within a few years a single plant becomes a thriving colony if its soil is enriched with bone-meal and peat.*

| PLANT | IN FLOWER | COLOURS |
| --- | --- | --- |
| Achillea (H) | Summer | Pink, yellow |
| Agapanthus (H) | Summer | Blue, white |
| Alstroemeria (H) | Summer | Orange, pink, red |
| Anemone (H) | Summer, autumn | Pink, red, white |
| Artemisia (H) | Summer | Foliage: silvery white |
| Berberis (S) | Spring | Orange, yellow |
| Bergenia (H) | Spring | Pink, red, white |
| Buddleia (S) | Summer | Blue, mauve, red, white |
| Carpenteria (S) | Summer | White |
| Caryopteris (S) | Summer, autumn | Blue |
| Catananche (H) | Summer | Blue |
| Ceanothus (S) | Spring, summer | Blue, pink |
| Centaurea (H) | Summer | Blue, pink |
| Choisya (S) | Spring, autumn | White |
| Chrysanthemum (H) | Autumn | Various |
| Cistus (S) | Summer | Pink, red, white, yellow |
| Clematis (C) | Spring, summer, winter | Various |
| Cotoneaster (S) | Summer | White; red berries |
| Crocosmia (H) | Summer | Orange, red, yellow |
| Cytisus (S) | Spring | Purple, red, white, yellow |
| Dianthus (H) | Summer | Pink, red, white |
| Dierama (H) | Summer | Pink, purple, white |
| Eccremocarpus (C) | Summer | Orange, red |
| Echinops (H) | Summer | Blue |
| Elaeagnus (S) | — | Foliage: variegated |
| Endymion (B) | Spring | Blue, pink, white |
| Erigeron (H) | Summer | Blue, orange, pink |
| Eryngium (H) | Summer | Blue |
| Escallonia (S) | Summer | Pink, red, white |
| *Euonymus japonicus* | — | Foliage: green or variegated |
| Euphorbia (H) | Spring, summer | Lime, orange, yellow |
| Festuca (H) | — | Foliage: blue-grey |
| Fremontia (S) | Summer | Yellow |
| Fuchsia (S) | Summer, autumn | Pink, red, white |
| Garrya (S) | Winter | Silver catkins |
| Gazania (H) | Summer | Orange, yellow |
| Genista (S) | Spring, summer | Yellow |
| Geranium (H) | Summer | Blue, pink, red, white |
| Gypsophila (H) | Summer | White |
| Hebe (S) | Summer | Blue, pink, purple, red |
| Hedera (S) | — | Foliage: variegated |
| Heuchera (H) | Spring, summer | Pink, red |

| PLANT | IN FLOWER | COLOURS |
|---|---|---|
| Hibiscus (S) | Summer, autumn | Blue, mauve, red, white |
| Hydrangea (S) | Summer, autumn | Blue, pink, red, white |
| Hypericum (S) | Summer | Yellow |
| Iris (H) | Spring | Various |
| Juniperus (S) | — | Foliage: blue, green, grey, yellow |
| Kniphofia (H) | Summer | Orange, red, yellow |
| Lathyrus (C) | Summer | Pink, red, white |
| Lavandula (S) | Summer | Blue, purple |
| Lavatera (S) | Summer | Pink, red |
| Leycesteria (S) | Summer, autumn | Red/white; purple berries |
| Linaria (A), (H) | Summer | Pink, violet |
| Lychnis (H) | Summer | Pink, red |
| Myrtus (S) | Summer | White |
| Oenothera (H) | Summer | Yellow |
| Olearia (S) | Summer | White |
| Osmanthus (S) | Spring | White |
| Passiflora (C) | Summer | Blue/white |
| Penstemon (H), (S) | Summer | Blue, pink, red |
| Phormium (S) | — | Foliage: sword-like leaves |
| Polygonum (H) | Summer | Cream, pink, red |
| Potentilla (S) | Summer | Cream, yellow |
| Primula vulgaris and hybrids (H) | Spring | Various |

| PLANT | IN FLOWER | COLOURS |
|---|---|---|
| Pyracantha (S) | Summer | White; red or yellow berries |
| Ribes (S) | Spring | Pink, red |
| Romneya (S) | Summer | White, yellow |
| Rosmarinus (S) | Spring | Blue |
| Sambucus (S) | Spring, summer | Cream; cut foliage; black or red fruits |
| Santolina (S) | Summer | Yellow; silvery leaves |
| Scabiosa (H) | Summer | Mauve, pink, white, yellow |
| Scilla (B) | Spring, autumn | Blue, white |
| Sedum (H) | Summer | Pink, red |
| Skimmia (S) | Spring | White; red berries |
| Solanum (C) | Summer | Blue, purple |
| Spartium (S) | Summer | Yellow |
| Symphoricarpos (S) | — | White or pink fruits |
| Tamarix (S) | Summer | Pink |
| Tradescantia (H) | Summer | Blue, red, violet |
| Tropaeolum (C) | Summer | Orange, red, yellow |
| Veronica (H) | Summer | Blue |
| Viburnum tinus (S) | Winter, spring | Pinkish white |
| Weigela (S) | Spring | Pink |
| Yucca (S) | Summer | White |

| (B) = Bulb | (H) = Herbaceous |
|---|---|
| (C) = Climber | (S) = Shrub |

*Known as elephant's ears on account of its large leathery leaves, Bergenia 'Ballawley' is a robust member of the clan and its spring-flowering stems grow 600–750 mm (2–2½ ft) high in heavy, moist soil.*

# HEIGHT, SPREAD & SHAPE

*When planning a mixed border aim at creating an interesting network of varying shapes, textures and heights of shrubs, herbaceous perennials and annuals. Plant a focal point – such as the flowering tree in this picture – and then encourage the eye to wander easily among carefully contoured plantings.*

When you plan your flower garden, think carefully about the various elements in the total scheme and how they will relate to each other. There is, for instance, a great and obvious contrast between the hard, angular lines and solid mass of the house and the slender, flowing shapes of flowering plants. The visual transition from one to the other can be made less abrupt in many ways – by training climbers on the house walls, for instance, or by extending paving outward from the house and stocking it with container plants. In the same way, different parts of the garden can be made to merge into one another, the eye being led from one to the next by carefully sited visual 'signals' – a decorative urn, perhaps, or stepping stones curving across the margins of a lawn.

The view from the house windows is important, especially in winter. Here flowers come into their own, whether they are herbaceous plants, bulbs, flowering shrubs or roses. When you are choosing them, their season of flowering, as well as their colours, are important.

### VARYING THE LEVELS

A variation in levels and a variation of plant heights all help to add interest; for instance, a herbaceous border can all too easily have a single horizontal level. Break it up with the smaller, vertically growing conifers, juniper 'Skyrocket', the fastigiate Irish yew or evening primroses (*Oenothera*). Use shrubs as a change from herbaceous plants; go in for bulbs – these can vary from the tiny front-of-border snowdrops and crocuses to the 900 mm (3 ft) crown imperials and summer hyacinths (*Galtonia*).

The herbaceous border, when first conceived, contained plants graded in height so that the lowest were in front and the tallest at the back; it was meant to be looked at from only one side. When successful it was superb, but it was difficult to achieve and often difficult to cultivate. The modern idea has commuted this a little to the 'island border'. This is a bed of irregular curving shape, cut in turf or surrounded by paving, containing perennials arranged so that the tallest are more or less in the middle, and the carpeters at the edges. The shapes of these beds can be very pleasing and, being islands, they are more easily cared for, particularly if no-staking perennials are grown.

This last point is not to be overlooked in planting. The more time you have to spare, the more you can improve the garden, and enjoy it, too; a garden which is always needing attention becomes a tiresome job which has to be done, instead of being a place for pleasure and interest, as it should be. Shrubs are plants which do not need a lot of care, on the whole, but which can provide much in the way of flowers, fruits and foliage. Ground-cover plants will fill in spaces between perennials and shrubs so that the weeds cannot spread; ivy, periwinkle, heathers, London pride, St John's wort (*Hypericum*), creeping thyme and saxifrages, once established, need virtually no attention.

## LAYING OUT A MIXED BORDER

The size, shape and levels of a mixed flower border will be largely influenced by the existing site. Depth and breadth of the bed should be taken into account as much as the proposed colour schemes and season of interest, and the height and character of the plants should relate to each other and their surroundings.

A simple plan for a border in front of a hedge could have tall plants placed at the back and shorter subjects to the fore. With large borders it is better to set plants in groups rather than individually, or a spotty effect may be created. Tall spiky plants like delphiniums and verbascum contrast well with round-headed flowers like achillea and phlox, or with plants such as helenium that form a mounded clump.

The duration and times of the flowering season are important: borders close to the house need subjects that provide year-round colour, although a traditional herbaceous border usually has a short but splendid season in summer. Small evergreen shrubs introduced in a mixed border provide a useful framework and give year-round interest.

Strong hues of red or yellow contrast well against shades of green and blue. White and cream blend harmoniously with most flower colours. Bronze, orange and pinks create a warm effect, compared with the coolness of blues and lavenders. Grey foliage blends or contrasts with red, cerise, pink and white shades.

**Above** *A handsome raised trough such as this creates interest for much of the year, especially in spring and early summer. It can feature permanent plant residents or be used to display a changing parade of colourful bedding plants.*

**Left** *The stately evening primrose* (Oenothera) *makes a handsome sentinel to punctuate a border and elevate an otherwise flattish planting scheme. This one is* O. tetragona '*Fireworks*'.

**Berberis darwinii**
*Evergreen. April flowers followed by berries. Any soil; open site. Height 1.8–2.4 m (6–8 ft).*

**Euonymus japonicus 'Aureus'** *Evergreen. Well-drained soil; sunny site. Height 3–4.5 m (10–15 ft).*

**Daisy bush**
(Olearia × haastii)
*Evergreen shrub. Scented flowers in July. Prune in spring. Well-drained, fertile soil; full sun. Height 1.2 m (4 ft).*

# THE BACKCLOTH

## SHRUBS

An herbaceous or mixed border of shrubs and hardy perennials needs a contrasting backcloth – a wall, fence, hedge or informal arrangement of evergreen trees or shrubs.

A yew (*Taxus*) or arbor-vitae (*Thuja*) hedge is ideal. Clipped once a year, in August, it doesn't grow out of hand and the deep-green foliage contrasts superbly with the orange-red tones of crocosmia and kniphofia, the sun-yellow blooms of achillea and helianthus, and the snow-white of the bellflower (*Campanula lactiflora* 'Alba').

Other evergreen shrubs include berberis, attractive and easy-to-grow. One of the best is the charming *B. darwinii*. Californian lilacs (*Ceanothus*) are blue-flowered shrubs which bloom in spring, summer or autumn.

Another very attractive flowering shrub is Mexican orange blossom (*Choisya ternata*). Grown mostly for the beauty of their foliage, *Elaeagnus* are hardy, with tiny, scented flowers in spring or autumn. The oleaster (*E. commutata*) has deciduous silver leaves and bears small, silvery fruits.

Escallonia grow particularly well in seaside gardens. *E. × edinensis* has pink flowers in arching sprays; *E. ×* 'Apple Blossom' pink and white, 'Donard Brilliance', crimson. All flower in June–July. Another good shrub for seaside gardens is *Euonymus japonicus* 'Aureus', with glossy, gold-centred leaves.

Yet another good hedging and backcloth plant for seaside gardens (and towns) is the daisy bush (*Olearia*). Probably the best is the hybrid *O. × haastii*, whose flattish clusters of daisy-like flowers bloom in July.

*Osmanthus delavayi*, a rounded evergreen shrub, has strongly scented small white flowers in April, and small glossy, dark green leaves.

The firethorns (*Pyracantha*) are evergreen in reasonable winters, and very spiny. They are quite hardy and grown mostly for their fruits.

Most garden senecios have grey or silvery foliage and yellow flowers in summer and early autumn. The best garden species is *Senecio* 'Sunshine', whose leaves are white-felted.

## HERBACEOUS PLANTS

Point up your medium-size and low-growing border plants with a backcloth of tall, elegant herbaceous types, preferably self-supporting up to a height of 1.5 m (5 ft) to 2 m (6½ ft), depending on the size of the border.

Delphiniums, reliable and popular herbaceous border plants in English gardens, are also among the most handsome; they contribute some of the most vivid blues to the garden scene. The blues of the large-flowered hybrids show infinite variation, from the palest powder blue to deepest navy, with violet, lilac, mauve and pink tingeing the petals; white, cream and yellow are also represented. Outstanding amongst the magnificent Pacific Hybrids, which reach at least 1.8 m (6 ft) high, are the blue 'Ann Page', pink 'Astolat', and white 'Pacific Galahad'. The Belladonna cultivars are smaller, and with looser

The plume poppy (*Macleaya microcarpa*) is quite unlike a poppy in its flowers. It is a tall plant whose habit of growth provides a welcome airiness amongst the denser foliage and flowers of most perennials. The large rounded, scalloped-edged leaves have silvery undersides; the small, yellowish buff-coloured flowers grow in large feathery clusters at the top of each stem.

## Herbaceous Plants

| NAME | DESCRIPTION | HEIGHT/ SPREAD | IN FLOWER | SOIL AND SITE | REMARKS | PROPAGATION |
|---|---|---|---|---|---|---|
| **Acanthus spinosus** bear's breeches | Distinctive, deeply cut foliage and spectacular spikes of mauve-purple flowers | H: 1.2 m (4 ft) S: 600 mm (2 ft) | July–Sept | Deep, well-drained loam, sunny or slightly shaded | Dislikes disturbance | Root cuttings in Jan. or Feb. Large clumps can be divided between Oct. and April |
| **Achillea** | Attractive divided foliage, and flat yellow flower-heads. 'Coronation Gold' (deep yellow; H: 0.9–1.2 m/ 3–4 ft, S: 750–900 mm/ 2½–3 ft); 'Moonshine' (silvery foliage, pale yellow flowers; H: 600 mm/2 ft, S: 45 cm/1½ ft) | See description | June–Aug | Stony, gravelly or chalky soils, full sun | Trouble-free plants in right conditions. Flower-heads retain colour for many months when cut and dried | Divide established clumps in Sept. or spring. Keep young plants moist until established |
| **Alstroemeria ligtu Hybrids** Peruvian lily | Small lily-like flowers. Pink, scarlet, orange and yellow | H: 60–90 cm (2–3 ft) S: 300 mm (1 ft) | June–Aug. | Fertile, well-drained soil, sheltered from cold winds | Always plant pot-grown specimens: root disturbance resented | Divide established clumps in spring. Raised from seed |

| NAME | DESCRIPTION | HEIGHT/ SPREAD | IN FLOWER | SOIL AND SITE | REMARKS | PROPAGATION |
|------|-------------|----------------|-----------|---------------|---------|-------------|
| *Artemisia lactiflora* white mugwort | Plumes of fragrant creamy-white flowers, deeply divided leaves | H: 1.2 cm (4 ft) S: 600 mm (2 ft) | Aug.–Oct. | Well-drained soil, sun or part shade | In autumn, cut plants down to soil level | Divide clump from Oct. to March |
| *Campanula lactiflora* bellflower | Light blue bells 25 mm (1 in) across on tall, leafy stems. Cultivars include 'Loddon Anna' (lilac-pink) | H: 1.2 m (4 ft) S: 900 mm (3 ft) | June–Aug. | Fertile, well-drained soil, sun or partial shade | Support may be necessary in windy areas | Divide in March or April |
| *Delphinium* (garden hybrids) | Many good cultivars: 'Ann Page' (semi-double, cornflower blue), 'Black Knight' (dark blue), 'King Arthur' (purple, with white eye) and 'Startling' (deep violet, white eye) | H: 1.8 m (6 ft) S: 750–900 mm (2½–3 ft) | June–Aug. | Deep fertile soil, sunny position, sheltered from strong winds | Staking essential. After flowering, cut stems back to soil level. | Take cuttings in April. Root in equal parts peat and sand in a cold-frame. Divide established plants in spring. Raised from seed. |
| *Eupatorium purpureum* joe-pye weed | Clustered heads of purple-crimson flowers | H: 1.5 m (5 ft) S: 900 m (3 ft) | Aug.–Sept. | Ordinary soil, sun or partial shade | Ensure soil is kept moist. Cut foliage down to ground in autumn | Divide in Oct. or March |
| *Helianthus* 'Loddon Gold' perennial sunflower | Double, golden-yellow flowers | H: 1.5 m (5 ft) S: 1 m (3¼ ft) | Aug.–Sept. | Well-drained soil, full sun | May need support in exposed places | Divide in Oct. or April |
| *Inula magnifica* | Very large, with hoary leaves, bright yellow daisy-like blooms | H: 1.8 m (6 ft) S: 900 mm (3 ft) | July–Aug. | Moisture-retentive soil, full sun | Ensure plants do not become dry | Divide in March or April |
| *Kniphofia* (garden hybrids) red-hot poker | Stiff spikes in shades of glowing orange, red or yellow | H: 1–1.2 m (3½–4 ft) S: 450 mm (1½ ft) | June–July | Good soil, full sun | Plant in Sept or Oct, mulch in spring | Divide established plants in April |
| *Ligularia dentata* (syn. *L. clivorum*, *Senecio clivorum*) | 'Desdemona' has large, vivid orange daisy-like heads and large flushed purple leaves | H: 1.2 m (4 ft) S: 900 mm (3 ft) | July–Sept. | Moist, deeply cultivated soil, full sun | May require support and protection from winds | Divide established plants in April |
| *Macleaya cordata* (syn. *Bocconia cordata*) plume poppy | Creamy-white, 12 mm (½ in) long flowers carried in sprays above lobed, glaucous leaves | H: 1.2 m (4 ft) S: 900 mm (3 ft) | Aug.–Sept. | Deep soil, sunny but sheltered position | Support young growth with twiggy sticks | Divide established plants from Oct. to April |
| *Sidalcea* | Spires of attractive mallow-like pink flowers. Cultivars include 'Pink Pinnacle' (clear pink), 'Rose Queen' (clear rose), and 'William Smith' (salmon) | H: 1.2 m (4 ft) S: 600 mm (2 ft) | June–Aug. | Ordinary garden soil, full sun | Cut flowering stems down to 300 mm (1 ft) immediately after blooming | Divide in spring. Can also be grown from seed |

**Far left** Osmanthus delavayi's *arching shoots are clad with scented tubular white flowers in April and May. It reaches a height and spread of up to 6 m (20 ft).*

**Near left** *Possessing great charm, 'Pink Sensation' – one of the Belladonna group of delphiniums – looks superb in front of cream-coloured climbers. It grows up to 1.3 m (4½ ft) high.*

### CLIMBERS & TRAILERS

You can almost double the potential growing space of your patio or garden if you use the boundary walls or fences in an imaginative way. Climbers on the walls of a house, for instance, can turn them into part of the garden scheme and bring flowers close to the windows. Climbers can also be used to hide unsightly items.

A climber can be used to frame a window. Morning glory (*Ipomoea*), grown in pots, for instance, can be trained up lines of twine around the window. Or you can build a narrow trellis and grow climbers up that. Even a humble chain-link fence can have a climber, such as common ivy (*Hedera helix*), trained and tied to it so that it is completely covered and becomes a lush green 'wall'.

A warm and sheltered wall, which usually retains heat either from the house or from the sun can be used to give protection to the more tender plants which might perish if grown in the open. Climbers trained to scale a post, archway or pergola can provide an accent or a focal point. Similarly, an ugly dead tree can be turned into an object of beauty if it has an attractive plant growing over it.

Climbing shrubs do not always have to be grown upwards: training them in the reverse direction can be decorative as well as useful. A somewhat plain bank can be covered effectively by planting several climbers at the top and allowing them to trail downwards.

Some evergreens should be included in a planting scheme of this type to ensure that walls and fences do not become bare in winter. During the summer, when flower-beds are blooming, it is not so important to plant climbers on the boundaries to give bright colours. In winter, however, when most plants are bare, some winter- or autumn-flowering climbers and wall plants give great pleasure. Examples are flowering quince (*Chaenomeles speciosa*), which has rosy red flowers in January, at least in mild winters; its cultivar 'Aurora', which has salmon-pink blooms in October; the winter sweet (*Chimonanthus praecox*), which has sweetly scented, pale yellow flowers from December to February; and *Clematis cirrhosa balearica*, which produces pale yellow blossoms, spotted reddish purple, throughout the winter.

Climbing roses should be sited with care if space is restricted, as their prickles may become a nuisance. They grow best of all on open trellis or laths set slightly away from a brick wall,

*Typical planting scheme for the backcloth, with the tallest plants trained against a wall. Key to numbers: 1 Delphinium, 2 Passion-flower (Passiflora), 3 Yarrow (Achillea), 4 Red-hot poker (Kniphofia), 5 Trumpet vine (Campsis), 6 Garrya elliptica, 7 Shrubby euphorbia, 8 Clematis, 9 Day lily (Hemerocallis), 10 Bellflower (Campanula).*

because they need plenty of air around them to discourage the scourge of mildew. For a small wall the 'Lemon Pillar' rose (which is in fact white) or 'Crimson Coral Satin' is a good choice. If you prefer pink, 'Conrad F. Meyer', a rugosa rose, is a pretty one to choose. Ramblers, on the other hand, behave exactly as their name suggests – ramble all over the place and are not so suitable for a small area.

Clematis and other 'softer' climbers, such as winter jasmine (*Jasminum nudiflorum*) and honeysuckle (*Lonicera*) will need plenty of wirenetting or trellis to cling to and climb over and to protect them from strong winds. But they do tend to make fast growth and flower quickly and they do not need tying in. They can also be grown easily in pots, as can the passion flower (*Passiflora caerulea*), which actually flowers better if it has some root restriction.

If you are planning on climbers for pergolas and posts around a terrace, a vine, traditionally, makes an attractive network of leaves under which to dine out or sit. The most vigorous variety to choose is *Vitis vinifera* 'Brandt', which has foliage that colours in the autumn and tempting dark red grapes that can be used for desserts or for making wine.

If you have a wall, or an unsightly building that you want to cover rapidly, then the fastest, most vigorous climber you are likely to come across is Russian vine (*Polygonum baldschuanicum*), which can cover 6 m (20 ft) of wall in one season. However, the trouble is that once having started it, it is difficult to get it to stop. It is deciduous, too, so you are left with bare branches in winter. But if judiciously clipped and pruned back, it quite quickly forms a thick network of trunks which makes it an attractive proposition for, say, a pergola where you want leaves overhead; and its long delicate racemes of white flowers hang down in an attractive way. It is a good choice to compensate for a slower-growing, more attractive climber like a vine or wisteria, provided you keep it under control. Two other rapid climbers to look for are *Clematis montana* varieties and *Rosa filipes* 'Kiftsgate', a very vigorous rambler with white flowers that will eventually need checking. Clematis can also be used to scramble over an existing bush or tree. More instant cover is provided by the perennial climbing nasturtium, Scottish Flame (*Tropaeolum speciosum*), which grows fast while permanent climbers are becoming established.

Tall plants to consider putting against a wall to brighten it up on a temporary basis include sunflowers (*Helianthus annuus*), tall delphiniums, foxgloves (*Digitalis purpurea*), hollyhocks (*Althaea rosea*), and black-eyed susan (*Rudbeckia hirta*).

North walls can be a problem, but fortunately there are a number of attractive climbers that will cope with them, notably *Hydrangea petiolaris*. This bears little or no resemblance to the ordinary hydrangea, having delicate lace-like white flowers and dark, glossy green leaves; it reaches a height of 14 m (46 ft).

Do not be tempted to choose the tallest plant in the garden centre: take a good hard look at it first for it may be drawn out and straggly. A climber that is shorter but has several stems may be a better bet and will soon catch up in height when it is in the ground. If it is container-grown, make sure that it is not pot-bound (that is, with overcrowded roots).

*Captivating daisy-like blooms of the coneflower or black-eyed-susan (Rudbeckia hirta) are borne freely on sturdy stems in early autumn when the main summer display of border plants has dwindled. Contrasting effectively with a red brick wall, it is perfect for planting close to the house.*

### CLIMBERS FOR A SUNNY WALL

Wisterias are among the most showy and colourful climbing shrubs. They support themselves by twining stems, and their long tassels of pea flowers, lilac purple in most forms, are a magnificent sight in May and June. *Wisteria sinensis* is the most popular species, with flower clusters 200–300 mm (8–12 in) long. These appear before the leaves. The white form, 'Alba', is also well worth growing. *W. floribunda*, the Japanese wisteria, has the most striking cultivar of all, 'Macrobotrys', with pendant lilac flower trusses up to 1 m (3¼ ft) long. Wisteria flowers have a spicy scent, reminiscent of lupins.

Summer jasmine (*J. officinale*) is a vigorous twiner which produces masses of small white, intensely fragrant flowers from June to September. Its rather untidy and straggling habit of growth makes it most suitable for growing through trees or over sheds or other outbuildings.

Honeysuckles (*Lonicera*) are grown as much for their perfume as for their decorative display. Cultivars of our native woodbine (*L. periclymenum*) are among the most fragrant, although some other species and hybrids are showier and more colourful.

### SELF-SUPPORTING CLIMBERS

Most garden climbers attach themselves to supports by means of twining stems or leaf tendrils. A few, however, require no support, gripping walls or other vertical surfaces with aerial roots or self-clinging pads. The following are typical self-supporters.

North American trumpet vine (*Campsis radicans*), a deciduous shrub, has light green leaves, and in August and September produces brilliant orange and scarlet, trumpet-shaped flowers. It grows to a height of about 12 m (40 ft) and likes enriched, well-drained soil in shelter and full sun. The much less vigorous *C. × tagliabuana* 'Madame Galen' has large, pink-red trumpets.

Among the ivies the Canary Island form (*Hedera canariensis* 'Gloire de Marengo') is a rapid-growing evergreen with leathery leaves, dark green in the centre, becoming silvery grey

and then white at the margin. Older leaves are sometimes flecked crimson. Thrives in any soil in sun or shade but is not hardy in severe winters. It grows to about 6 m (20 ft) and needs pruning to keep it in bounds.

Persian ivy (*H. colchica*) is strong and quick-growing, with dark green leaves, glossy and leathery and grows in any soil. Needs pruning in

**Right** *Scented early or late Dutch honeysuckle (Lonicera periclymenum) is perfect for draping a pergola or cascading from a patio's overhead beams. Happy in sun or light shade, it flowers in July–September.*

**Passion flower** (Passiflora caerulea) *Climbs by means of leaf tendrils; best for a south- or west-facing wall. Yellow, egg-shaped fruits follow flowers. Height 3–4 m (10–13 ft). Take stem cuttings in July–August.*

**Trumpet vine** (Campsis radicans) *Self-clinging by aerial roots; likes a sunny wall. 'Madame Galen' is an impressive salmon-red flowered cultivar. Height 6–7 m (20–23 ft). Take semi-hardwood cuttings in August.*

**Virginia creeper** (Parthenocissus quinquefolia) *Makes a vivid curtain of autumn tinted leaves. Climbs by limpet-like sucker discs. Height 7–8 m (23–26 ft). Take hardwood cuttings in November.*

late winter to control its size. Height 7.5 m (25 ft). Its variety 'Dentata Variegata' has large, shiny leaves soft green in colour with marked, deep yellow variegations; and grows to less than half the height.

Common ivy (*H. helix*) is a hardy evergreen with glossy dark green leaves. Happy in any soil, it needs pruning to control shape and size. Height 30 m (100 ft). Its varieties 'Buttercup', 'Golden Cloud' and 'Russell's Gold' have small, yellow, evergreen leaves, and are very slow-growing; 'Purpurea' has small evergreen leaves, green-coloured during the summer, turning deep purple in inter; 'Sagittaefolia Variegata' has small, evergreen leaves, shaped like an arrow-head with creamy white markings.

Climbing hydrangea (*Hydrangea petiolaris*) is deciduous and strong-growing, with rich, dark green, serrated leaves, pale green and downy underneath and turning lemon-coloured in autumn, and reddish-brown, peeling bark. Produces white flowers in June. Thrives on a north wall. Height 15 m (50 ft).

Chinese Virginia creeper (*Parthenocissus henryana*) is deciduous and not quite hardy. Its dark green leaves, with white and pink veinal variegations, turn red in autumn. Height 9 m (30 ft).

True Virginia creeper (*P. quinquefolia*) is hardy and deciduous, with green leaves that change to bright orange and red in autumn. Grows in moist, rich soil. Needs pruning in summer to control its denseness and spread. Height 21 m (70 ft).

## ROSES

Apart from *Rosa filipes* 'Kiftsgate', already mentioned, there are many attractive roses suitable for growing against vertical supports. They can be divided into three main types. The first are the large-flowered climbers, of which the following are typical: 'Aloha' yields large, very full, fragrant flowers, deep rose-pink suffused with orange-salmon, from June onwards. Excellent for small gardens; moderately vigorous, it will grow on a north wall to a height of 1.8 m (6 ft). 'Casino' is repeat-flowering, has soft yellow, very fragrant flowers that open from deeper yellow buds, and dark green foliage. Vigorous and grows to a height of 2.7 m (9 ft). 'Compassion' has pale salmon-orange flowers with apricot shading that is lighter on the reverse. They are full and very fragrant and appear from June onwards. Very vigorous, grows to a height of 3 m (10 ft). 'Danse de Feu' produces full blooms of bright orange-red from June throughout the summer. Moderately vigorous, it will grow on a north wall and reaches a height of 2.4 m (8 ft). 'Parkdirektor Riggers' has dark green leaves and blood-red, semi-double, recurrent flowers borne in clusters from mid-June onwards. It will grow

on a north wall and is vigorous, reaching a height of 3.5 m (12 ft).

Rambler roses have vigorous but looser growth than the climbers but can readily be trained to take up the shape of their supports.

Four good ones are: 'Albéric Barbier', a veteran, having been introduced in 1900, with white, yellow-centred, fragrant flowers in June. The shiny foliage is semi-evergreen. Grows to a height of 7.5 m (25 ft). 'Crimson Shower' has clusters of small, rosette flowers in July and August. Vigorous; grows to a height of 2.4 m (8 ft). 'Emily Gray' has golden-buff, scented blooms in early summer, and semi-evergreen foliage. Very vigorous: grows to a height of 3.5 m (12 ft). 'New Dawn' is a repeat-flowering rambler with pale flesh-pink, full, perfumed flowers. Moderately vigorous: grows to 3 m (10 ft).

Sprawling roses are particularly good for covering tree stumps, training up steep banks, or using as ground cover. Two recommended varieties: 'Max Graf', a modern hybrid Rugosa shrub, has bright pink, single flowers with white centres and golden stamens in mid- to late-June. Vigorous and trailing, it reaches a height of 300 mm (1 ft). Good for quick ground-cover. 'Nozomi' has trusses of pearl-pink, single flowers. It has a spreading habit and will extend to a width of 600 mm (2 ft). Unsupported it grows to a height of 450 mm (1½ ft); supported it will grow up to 1.5 m (5 ft).

**Above** *Roses around a door (or a window) evoke cottage-garden tranquillity. There are dozens of repeat-flowering climbers and ramblers to choose from. Dead-head them regularly to encourage strong new shoots and a recurrent display of blooms.*

## THE CENTRE

The middle of a border should dominate. Plants chosen for their shape and leaf texture, compatible colours and longevity of bloom should be the focus of an admiring and critical eye. The plants you choose should be about 450–750 mm (1½–2½ ft) high and carefully graded so that the smaller are not overshadowed by the larger.

### HERBACEOUS PERENNIALS

The following are a few among many species of excellent permanent residents.

The deciduous African lilies (*Agapanthus*) have proved to be surprisingly hardy, considering their country of origin. Clusters of blue, bell-like flowers 50 mm (2 in) wide, appear at the top of stems 600–900 mm (2–3 ft) long from July to September. The strap-shaped leaves are profusely produced in a long arching rosette at the base of the plant from fleshy, rather brittle roots. The Headbourne Hybrids have a good range of blues, from sky-blue to deep blue and violet-blue. African lilies prefer a sunny site and rich but well-drained soil.

Among the astilbes the garden hybrids grouped under *A. × arendsii* are most commonly seen nowadays. They are erect, bushy plants with finely divided, fern-like leaves – some tinged bronze or purple – and sprays of tiny flowers in June–August. Good examples of medium-sized forms are 'Fire' (salmon-red), 'Irrlicht' (white), and 'Ostrich' (pink). All these grow to about 750 mm (2½ ft) in height.

The masterwort (*Astrantia carniolica*), 600 mm (2 ft), popular with flower-arrangers, has white pink-tinged flowers in July–August. *A. major* has similarly starlike flowers, but greenish pink in colour; while in *A. maxima* the flowers are rich pink. Sun and light shade are equally suitable sites; any reasonably fertile soil will do.

There are several good varities of the Shasta daisy (*Chrysanthemum maximum*), with flowers comprising a yellow disc, and white rays. Typical are 'Everest', 'Mayfield Giant' and 'Wirral Supreme', all 600–900 mm (2–3 ft) tall.

Two good cultivars of baby's breath (*Gypsophila paniculata*) are 'Bristol Fairy' and 'Compacta Plena'. Both have large misty clusters of white flowers from June to August, and are particularly good for floral arrangements. They thrive in good soil in sun 90 cm (3 ft); 45 cm (1½ ft) respectively.

The sea hollies (*Eryngium*) are fascinating for their somewhat thistle-like prickly and spiny stiff leaves and stems, and their coned flowers with a prickly ruff of bracts round each. The overall colouring of the plants is silvery blue. *E. alpinum* grows to 600 mm (2 ft) tall and 300 mm (1 ft) wide; its variety 'Violetta' is blue to violet-blue, growing to about 750 mm (2½ ft) tall and 450 mm (1½ ft) wide. The original sea holly, *E. maritimum*, is native to Britain, so the plants are not difficult to grow, though they like a very well-drained, rather poor soil.

The cultivars of *Phlox paniculata* bloom between July and September and may reach a height of 1.2 m (4 ft). There are some marvellous colours amongst them and excellent examples are 'White Admiral', cherry-red 'Starfire', and lavender-blue 'Skylight'. Another excellent variety is pink *P. maculata* 'Alpha'. For late-summer flowering, border phlox are hard to beat, but they must be watered well to ensure plenty of blossom that will not fade quickly. Plants flourish in rich, fertile soil.

The 'Gainsborough' variety of mullein (*Verbascum × phoeniceum*) is a beauty. Its clear, light yellow spires of bloom rise to 900 mm (3 ft). Another, 'Pink Domino', has rose-coloured flowers that contrast well with the yellow forms.

*Ox-eye daisies (Chrysanthemum maximum) flower for weeks in summer and create an imposing focus. Use them to separate 'hot' colours, such as reds and purples. Happy in any soil, though more vigorous on heavy clay, they come in single and double flowers; some have attractive 'anemone' centres.*

### ELBOW ROOM

One of the commonest mistakes with perennials is to underestimate the amount of room they need. Any plant which grows in the same place year after year must be expected to become bigger. If, in the early days, you are afraid the bed will look empty, fill in with annuals. Do not, however, overcrowd the perennials, which need room to expand by bushing out. Crowding will create tall and spindly growths and weak stems. In general, gardeners who find a great deal of staking is necessary have only themselves to blame.

Be sure that your borders are wide enough. It is a good basic rule to have a border twice as wide as the height of the tallest plants that it is to contain. This means that for plants 1.5 m (5 ft) high (delphiniums, for example, can easily exceed this height), a bed at least 3 m (10 ft) wide is necessary. If your borders are much narrower than this you should consider widening them by any means possible.

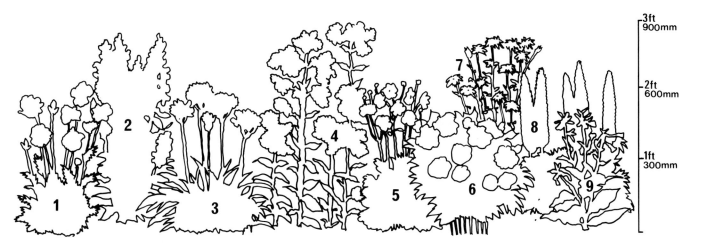

*Size and shape arrangements of plants suitable for the centre of the border, with a height range of 450–900 mm (1½–3 ft). Key to numbers: 1 Poppy (Papaver), 2 Antirrhinum, 3 African lily (Agapanthus), 4 Phlox, 5 Anemone, 6 Peony (Paeonia), 7 Chrysanthemum, 8 Lupin (Lupinus), 9 Tobacco plant (Nicotiana).*

## Herbaceous Perennials

| NAME | DESCRIPTION | HEIGHT/ SPREAD | IN FLOWER | SOIL AND SITE | REMARKS | PROPAGATION |
|------|-------------|----------------|-----------|---------------|---------|-------------|
| *Anchusa azurea* Alkanet | Brilliant blue flowers. Outstanding cultivar is 'Loddon Royalist' (H: 900 m/3 ft, S: 600 mm/2 ft) | See description | May–July | Deep, fertile soil, sunny position | Support with twigs | Root cuttings in Jan. or Feb. |
| *Aster novi-belgii* Michaelmas daisy | Good types: 'Ada Ballard' (mauve-blue, H: 900 mm/3 ft), 'Carnival' (semi-double, red, H: 600 mm/2 ft) | See description | Sept–Oct | Fertile soil, sunny position. Soil must not dry out during the flowering season | Tall cultivars may need twiggy supports. Replace with fresh stock every three years. | Divide in April or March |
| *Astrantia maxima* Masterwort | Star-like white or rose-pink flowers with greenish-pink bracts | H: 750 mm (2½ ft) S: 600 mm (2 ft) | June–July | Moist soil, shady or sunny | Staking may be necessary in exposed places | Divide between Oct. and March |
| *Anemone × hybrida* Japanese anemone | Magnificent for late flowering colour in the garden. Cultivars include 'Bressingham Glow' (rosy-red), 'September Charm' (pink and gold flowers), and 'White Queen' | H: 450– 900 mm (1½–3 ft) S: 300–600 mm (1–2 ft) | Aug–Oct | Fertile, moisture-retentive, well-drained soil, slight shade | May take a year or two to settle down. | Divide between Oct. and March |
| *Campanula persicifolia* Peach-leaved bellflower | Beautiful spires of blue or white flowers. 'Telham Beauty' is one of the best blues | H: 1 m (3¼ ft) S: 600 mm (2 ft) | June–Aug | Well drained, full or part sun | May need staking. Divide clumps in Oct. | |
| *Chrysanthemum maximum* Shasta daisy | Large white daisy flowers. 'Esther Read' (double, white) and 'Wirral Supreme' (large double white) are good | H: 900 mm (3 ft) S: 450 mm (1½ ft) | July–Sept | Best in well-drained soil in a sunny position | Divide clumps after three years | Divide established plants in spring |
| *Dicentra spectabilis* Bleeding heart | Drooping cascades of heart-shaped rosy-red flowers with white inner petals. Fern-like foliage | H: 600 mm (2 ft) S: 450 mm (1½ ft) | May–June | Rich, well drained soil, sheltered position | Trouble-freed, self-supporting plants | Divide in spring |
| *Erigeron* (garden hybrids) Fleabane | Like a low-growing and summer-flowering Michaelmas daisy. Cultivars include 'Amity' (lilac-pink), 'Charity' (clear pink), and 'Darkest of All' (violet-blue) | H: 600 mm (2 ft) S: 450 mm (1½ ft) | June–Aug | Moist, well-drained soil, full sun | Trouble-free plants | Divide established plants in spring or autumn |
| *Eryngium × oliverianum* Sea holly | Attractive, jagged-edged leaves, bright blue teasel-like flower-heads | H: 900 mm (3 ft) S: 750 mm (2½ ft) | June–Aug | Well-drained soil, full sun | Twiggy sticks may be necessary for support. Cut down in autumn | Take root cuttings in Feb., inserting in boxes of peat-sand in a cold-frame |

| NAME | DESCRIPTION | HEIGHT/ SPREAD | IN FLOWER | SOIL AND SITE | REMARKS | PROPAGATION |
|---|---|---|---|---|---|---|
| **Helenium** | Rayed flowers in shades of yellow, orange and red | H: 600–900 mm (2–3 ft) S: 450–600 mm (1½–2 ft) | July–Aug | Ordinary garden soil, full sun | Support in exposed positions | Divide in Oct or March |
| **Hemerocallis** (garden hybrids) Day lily | A long successfion of lily-like flowers in many colours. 'Black Magic' (ruby and purple), 'Buzz Bomb' (velvety-red), 'Fandango' (rich orange) | H: 600–900 mm (2–3 ft) S: 450 mm (1½ ft) | June–Sept | Good garden soil in a sun or part shade | Dislike disturbance | Divide in Oct or April |
| **Iris** (flag or German type) | Many superb cultivars, such as 'Berkeley Gold' (rich yellow), 'Braithwaite' (lavender standards, purple falls) and 'Jane Phillips' (flax blue) | H: 900 mm (3 ft) S: 450 mm (1½ ft) | May–June | Well-drained, sunny position. Lime is appreciated | Plant in late June or early July, with the rhizomes just below the surface | Divide old clumps immediately after flowering |
| **Lupinus** (garden hybrids) Lupin | Fine cultivars include 'My Castle' (brick-red), 'The Pages' (carmine), and 'The Governor' (blue and white) | H: 600–900 mm (2–3 ft) S: 450–600 mm (1½–2 ft) | June–July | Light soil, full sun or part shade. Avoid rich soil | Remove dead spikes after flowering | Cuttings in March or April. Sow seed in spring or summer |
| *Lychnis chalcedonica* Maltese cross | Spectacular plant with heads of brilliant scarlet flowes, shaped like a Maltese Cross | H: 900 mm (3 ft) S: 450 mm (1½ ft) | June–Aug | Ordinary garden soil, full sun or part shade | Support young growth with twigs. Mulch with peat or compost in spring | Raised from seed or by division. Cuttings 2.5–5 cm (1–2 in) long can be taken in April and rooted in a cold-frame |
| **Paeonia** (garden hybrids) Peony | Spectacular, like large, full, roses. Many cultivars, in shades of pink, red and white | H: 750–900 mm (2½–3 ft) S: 600 mm (2 ft) | June–Aug | Moist, rich, well-drained soil, sun or part shade | Mulch in spring. Support plants with stakes | Divide in Sept. |
| *Phlox paniculata* (garden hybrids) | Typical cultivars 'Dorothy Hanbury Forbes' (clear pink), 'Endurance' (salmon-orange), 'Prospero' (pale lilac), 'White Admiral' (white) | H: 900 mm (3 ft) S: 450 mm (1½ ft) | July–Sept. | Fertile, moisture-retentive soil, sun or part shade | Mulch annually in March or April. Water freely in dry weather | Divide in Oct. or April |
| *Salvia × superba* | Branching spires of violet-purple flowers | H: 900 mm (3 ft) S: 600 mm (2 ft) | July–Sept | Ordinary well-drained soil, full sun | Mulch with well-rotted compost in spring | Divide clumps in autumn or spring |

**African lily** (Agapanthus) *Deciduous evergreen perennials; Headbourne Hybrids are the hardiest forms. Well-drained, chalky soil preferred; full sun and sheltered site. Flowers in July and August. Height 900 mm (3 ft). Sow hybrid seeds in March–April.*

**Anemone × hybrida** *Early-autumn-flowering herbaceous perennial. Colonises well. Likes free-draining moist soil; light shade preferred. Height 1.2 m (4 ft). Take root cuttings in November–January.*

**Molly-the-witch peony** (Paeonia mlokosewitschii) *Herbaceous perennial. Flowers in April–May. Needs rich, moisture-retentive soil; sunny or lightly shaded site. Height 750 mm (2½ ft). Sow in September.*

*Astilbe × arendsii Herbaceous perennial hybrid. Sprays of tiny flowers in various colours in June–August. Cool, moist (even boggy) soil preferred; cool site. Height 450 mm–1.2 m (1½–4 ft). Increase by division in April.*

**Mullein** *(Verbascum × phoeniceum) Hardy herbaceous perennial hybrid. Tall, slender flower stems in June–August. Rich, well-drained soil; sunny, sheltered site. Height 1–2 m (3¼–6½ ft). Increase by root cuttings in February.*

**Cornflower** *(Centaurea cyanus) Hardy annual. Erect plant; flowers in various colours in summer. Likes fertile, well-drained soil; sunny site. Height up to 900 mm (3 ft). Sow in April or September.*

## BEDDING PLANTS

Although a mixed border consists principally of hardy perennials (herbaceous plants) and shrubs, there are usually gaps after the initial plantings and these may be filled with spring and summer bedding plants and bulbs.

There are many kinds of hardy annuals to choose from. Taller kinds from the focal, middle-of-the-border spot include the corncockle (*Agrostemma githago* 'Milas'), which sports soft lilac-pink or purple flowers on stems up to 1 m (3¼ ft) high; *Mentzelia lindleyi* (syn. *Bartonia aurea*), up to 600 mm (2 ft) high, with deep-lobed leaves and scented, saucer-shaped, golden flowers; tick weed (*Coreopsis drummondii* 'Golden Crown'), with golden yellow flowers with chestnut-brown centres. Others include *Chrysanthemum carinatum* 'Court Jesters', a vigorous grower to 600 mm (2 ft) with brightly zoned flowers in different colours; the graceful *Clarkia elegans* with its long spikes of salmon-pink, mauve, carmine or red flowers up to 600 mm (2 ft) high; and the Giant Imperial varieties of larkspur (*Delphinium consolida*), such as 'Blue Spire' (deep violet blue), 'White Spire', and 'Tall Hyacinth-Flowered'; the Spire forms grow to 1–1.2 m (3¼–4 ft) and the 'Hyacinth-Flowered' to 750–900 mm (2½–3 ft); the earlier, not quite so tall Stock-flowered group are also popular; 'Rosamund' is a bright pink variety.

The second group for summer bedding are the half-hardy annuals, of which the following are typical:

Love-lies-bleeding (*Amaranthus caudatus*) bears huge, showy, plum-red flower tassels in late summer; variety 'Viridis' has vivid green tassels. Cosmea (*Cosmos bipinnatus*), which grows up to 1.2 m (4 ft) high, has fern-like leaves and brightly coloured flowers up to 125 mm (5 in) in diameter in late summer or early autumn. The garden hybrid dahlias are among the most showy and popular hardies. Best-known of the bedding types are the 'Collerette Hybrids', which include single and double-flowered forms in single and mixed colours and grow to a height of 300–500 mm (12–20 in). The bells-of-Ireland or shell-flower (*Moluccella laevis*) is an intriguing-looking plant in which the tall spine carries tiny white flowers, each enclosed within light green bowl-shaped calyces. The spine is 750 mm (2½ ft) or more tall; it dries well and so is popular for winter-flower decorations. The velvet trumpet-flower (*Salpiglossis sinuata*), which reaches up to 600 mm (2 ft) in height, has pale green, narrow leaves and tall, graceful stems of trumpet-shaped red, pink, orange, gold, yellow or blue flowers from mid-summer to early autumn.

*Love-lies-bleeding (Amaranthus caudatus) impresses with its extraordinary flowering tassels. A half-hardy annual, it must be raised in heat in early spring and planted out when frosts finish.*

*Bred to withstand poor weather, Zinnia elegans 'Early Wonder' makes a stunning show from early summer to first frosts if fed regularly and watered in dry spells.*

### Bedding Plants

| NAME | DESCRIPTION | HEIGHT/ SPREAD | IN FLOWER | SOIL AND SITE | REMARKS | PROPAGATION |
|---|---|---|---|---|---|---|
| *Antirrhinum majus* Snapdragon | Half-hardy. Yellow, red, pink, orange, white: 'Madame Butterfly', 'Wedding Bells', 'Bright Butterflies' | H: 600– 900 mm (2–3 ft) S: 450 mm (1½ ft) | June–Oct | Rich, well-drained soil, sunny position | May require support | Sow under glass in Feb. or March. Plant out from late May onwards |
| | Medium-sized: 'Cheerio' (mixed), 'Coronette' (mixed), 'Little Darling' (mixed), 'Black Prince' (crimson, bronze leaves), 'Monarch' (mixed), 'Rembrandt' (orange, with gold tips) | H: 450 mm (1½ ft) S: 250 mm (10 in) | | | | |
| *Campanula medium* Canterbury bell | Biennial. Large bell-shaped flowers. Double and single-flowered sorts available in blue, mauve, rose, and white, growing to 750 mm (2½ ft) high and 450 mm (1½ ft) wide. There is also a 'Dwarf Bedding' mixture at 450 mm (1½ ft) high and 300 mm (1 ft) wide | See description | May–July | Fertile, well-drained soil, sunny position | Keep ground free of weeds during early stages of growth | Sow outdoors from April to June, and set the plants 15 cm (6 in) apart in nursery beds before moving to the flowering positions in Sept or Oct |
| *Centaurea cyanus* Cornflower | Hardy annual. 'Polka Dot', 450 mm (1½ ft) high, 300 mm (1 ft) wide, in blue, red, purple, pink, white | See description | June–Sept | Fertile, well-drained soil, full sun | Support tall cultivars | Sow in April or Sept. where they are to flower |

| NAME | DESCRIPTION | HEIGHT/ SPREAD | IN FLOWER | SOIL AND SITE | REMARKS | PROPAGATION |
|---|---|---|---|---|---|---|
| *Chrysanthemum carinatum* (syn C. tricolor) Annual chrysanthemum | Hardy annual. Bright, daisy-like flowers, red, yellow or white banded with contrasting colours. Examples: 'Double Mixed', 'Merry Mixed', 'Monarch Court Jesters' | H: 450– 600 mm (1½–2 ft) S: 250–375 mm (10–15 in) | June–Sept | Fertile, well-drained soil, sunny position | Nip out growing tips to encourage bushiness. Good for cutting | Sow outdoors from March to May, where plants will flower |
| *Cosmos bipinnatus* Cosmea | Half-hardy annual. Thread-like leaves, pink, rose, crimson or white flowers. Examples: 'Candy stripe' (white, crimson-splashed), 'Gloria' (large, rose-pink), 'Sensation Mixed' | H: 450– 1200 mm (1½–4 ft) S: 600 mm (2 ft) | Aug–Sept | Poor, light dry soil, full sun or semi-shade | Support the plants with twiggy sticks. Remove dead flower heads | Sow in a greenhouse in March or April. Set out young plants from May onwards |
| *Gypsophila elegans* Baby's breath | Hardy annual. Dainty, graceful white flowers. 'Covent Garden' (white) is good cultivar; 'Rosea' is a pink form | H: 600 mm (2 ft) S: 450 mm (1½ ft) | May–Sept | Well-drained, alkaline soil, full sun | Support plants with twiggy sticks | Sow in March–May where the plants are to flower – for summer flowering; sow in Sept for spring flowers |
| *Helianthus annuus* Sunflower | Hardy annual. 'Tall Yellow' (H: 2.4 m/8 ft, S: 750–900 mm/2½–3 ft) produces enormous yellow flowers; 'Sunburst' (H: 1.2 m/4 ft, S: 450–600 mm/1½–2 ft) has medium-sized flowers, varying from primrose to bronze and maroon. | See description | Aug–Oct | Well-drained soil, sunny position | Stake tall cultivars | Sow in March–May where the plants are to flower |
| *Lavatera trimestris* Mallow | Hardy annual. Showy long-flowering plant. 'Silver Cup' (H: 600–900 mm/2–3 ft, S: 750 mm/2½ ft) has trumpet-shaped flowers of bright, deep pink | See description | July–Sept | Most garden soils, but avoid excessive richness; sunny, sheltered position | Seeds itself freely | Sow where the plants are to flower, from March to May |
| *Zinnia elegans* | Half-hardy annual. Zinnias resemble small dahlias in white, pink, orange, yellow, scarlet, crimson, purple. Typical is 'Giant Double Mixed' | H: 600– 750 mm (2–2½ ft) S: 300– 1450 mm (1–½ ft) | July–Sept | Fertile soil, warm, sunny position | Nip out growing tips to induce plants to branch | Sow March or april in heated greenhouse; plant out in late May. |

*Tulips, especially the flamboyant 'botanical varieties', are a highlight of spring, but it's important to plant bulbs no earlier than October or they will push through the soil prematurely and risk infection from tulip-fire disease.*

## BULBS

Although all but the smallest bulbs can be used in a bedding display, hyacinths and tulips are the most satisfactory and the latter can be used at the front of the centre of the border. Their flowers are symmetrical, show up boldly and look well from any angle.

Tulips, which are planted in October, can be had in a vast range of colours, many of them attractively marked or shaded with a second colour. The time of flowering will depend on the type chosen. Early Single and Early Double tulips bloom in April and are followed by the mid-season Mendel and Triumph divisions of cultivars in late April-May, to be succeeded in turn by the traditional Darwin and Cottage types in May. Unusual flower shapes are provided by the Fringed, Parrot, and Lily-flowered tulips, which also bloom in May.

## FRONT OF BORDER

### HERBACEOUS FAVOURITES

Lady's mantle (*Alchemilla mollis*) has very attractive pleated leaves, rounded in outline, and grey-green in colour. The star-shaped, lime-green flowers, appear in June-August. The plant looks especially effective if associated with grey or sand-coloured paving.

Michaelmas daisy (*Aster novi-belgii*) is a boon for the autumn, its blooms lighting up the border in September and October. Choose the dwarf forms that grow not more than about 300 mm (1 ft) high.

*Bergenia cordifolia* is a good evergreen perennial for the front of border, its rounded, glossy leaves contrasting well with other foliage. It produces lilac-rose heads mainly in March and April, but can start to flower in January.

Border pinks are hybrids of *Dianthus plumarius* (don't confuse them with the border carnations, which are mostly a little too tall for the front of the border). Good examples are 'Doris' (pale salmon pink), 'Excelsior' (pink), 'Mrs Sinkins' and 'Sam Barlow' (both white).

### BEDDING PLANTS: HALF-HARDY

The following front-of-border bedders will make a colourful show, but must be planted out only when all risk of frost is past.

The ageratums have hairy, heart-shaped leaves and mounds of small, fluffy flowers in June–October. The best forms are $F_1$ hybrids of *A. houstonianum* and include 'Bengali' (rose-carmine), 'Blue Danube' (blue), 'Ocean' (light blue), 'Summer Snow' (white). None is more than 250 mm (10 in) high.

The antirrhinums include many attractive forms for both the centre and the front of the border. Those for the latter are forms of the variety *A. majus* 'Pumilum', which rarely exceed 150 mm (6 in) in height. They include 'Delice' (pale apricot), 'Floral Carpet' (mixed), 'Pixie' (mixed), 'Trumpet Serenade' (mixed).

Marigolds are available in two main forms – African (*Tagetes erecta*) and French (*T. patula*). Most of the African varieties are too tall for the front of the border except for the dwarf forms, such as the double-flowered 'Inca Orange' and 'Inca Yellow', which are less than 300 mm (1 ft) high. The French varieties include 'Honeycomb', 'Naughty Marietta', 'Spanish Brocade' and 'Tiger Eyes'.

### BEDDING PLANTS: HARDY

The clarkias are graceful plants with sword-shaped leaves with flower-spikes bearing double or semi-double flowers in July–September. *C. pulchella* is best for the front of border.

California poppy (*Eschscholzia californica*) has fern-like grey-green foliage and delicate orange flowers; it is 300–600 mm (1–2 ft) high. Good cultivars include 'Ballerina' (pink, orange and yellow with white), 'Cherry Ripe' (cerise), and 'Monarch Mixed' (crimson, cream, orange, red and yellow). If these are too tall, try the cultivars of *E. caespitosa* – notably 'Sundew' (lemon yellow) and 'Miniature Primrose' – which are not more than 150 mm (6 in) high.

Godetias (close relatives of clarkias) are compact, with mid-green pointed leaves and trumpet shaped reddish purple flowers in June–August. Cultivars include 'Azalea-Flowered Mixed', 'Crimson Glow', 'Dwarf Bedding Mixed', 'Sybil Sherwood' (salmon pink edged with white); all are about 375 mm (15 in) tall.

*Plants for the front of the border, ranging in height from 100 to 400 mm (4–16 in). Key to numbers: 1 Alyssum, 2 Pelargonium, 3 Petunia, 4 Cyclamen, 5 Geranium, 6 Lobelia, 7 Linum, 8 Pink (Dianthus), 9 Ageratum, 10 Godetia.*

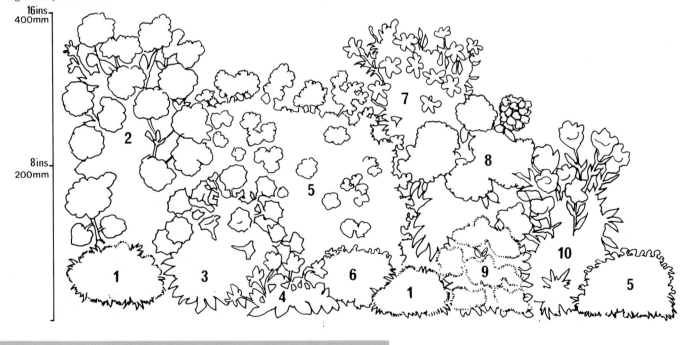

16ins
400mm

8ins
200mm

## Bedding Plants

| NAME | DESCRIPTION | HEIGHT/ SPREAD | IN FLOWER | SOIL AND SITE | REMARKS | PROPAGATION |
|------|-------------|----------------|-----------|---------------|---------|-------------|
| *Ageratum houstonianum* | Half-hardy annual. Heads of tiny blue powderpuff flowers | H: 150– 450 mm (6–8 in) S: 250–450 mm (10–18 in) | July–Oct | Moist soil, sheltered site | Remove dead flower heads to prolong flowering | Sow in warmth from Feb to April, and plant out from May onwards |
| *Anchusa capensis* Alkanet | Hardy annual. Resembles giant forget-me-not; a good cultivar is 'Blue Angel' (brilliant ultramarine) | H and S: 230–300 mm (9–12 in) | June–Sept | Deep, fertile and moist soil, full sun | Do not allow soil to become dry | Sow outdoors in March or April |
| *Begonia semperflorens* Bedding begonia | Half-hardy annual. Bushy tender perennial grown as half-hardy annual for bedding out. Flowers in shades of pink, red, and white. | H: 150– 230 mm (6–9 in) S: 150–230 mm (6–9 in) | June–Oct | Light, well-cultivated soil in full sun or part shade | After flowering plants should be discarded | Sow in late winter in a temperatue of 20–25°C (68–78°F), to produce plants large enough to bed out in late May |
| *Bellis perennis* Daisy | Biennial. Large, double, highly decorative forms of common daisy. Many cultivars | H: 100– 150 mm (4–6 in) S: 100–175 mm (4–7 in) | April–June | Fertile soil, sun or part shade | Dead-head plants to prevent them seeding | Sow 6 mm from April to June in cold-frame or outdoors; move to flowering positions in Sept or Oct |
| *Calendula officinalis* Pot marigold | Hardy annual. Bright, rayed pompon flowers in shades of orange or yellow. | H: 300– 600 mm (1–2 ft) S: 300–375 mm (1–1¼ ft) | May–Sept | Ordinary garden soil, good light. | Nip out terminal shoots to encourage branching; remove dead heads | Sow outdoors March–May for summer flowers, September for spring flowers |
| *Cheiranthus cheiri* Wallflower | Biennial. Fragrant spring bedding plants. Tall cultivars include 'Blood Red' (dark velvety crimson), 'Primrose Monarch' (primrose), and 'Ruby Gem' (violet-purple). Dwarf cultivars include 'Fair Lady' (charming mixture of pastel shades), and 'Tom Thumb' | H: 450 mm (1½ ft) S: 300 mm (1 ft) H: 230– 300 mm (9–12 in) S: 200–300 mm (8–12 in) | March–May | Alkaline soil, full sun | Protect young plants from cold winds | Sow in open ground during May–June; prick out seedlings in nursery rows. Plant in final positions as early as possible in autumn. |
| *Clarkia elegans* (syn. *C. unguiculata*) | Hardy annual. Graceful spikes of double flowers in shades of pink, red, mauve, purple, white | H: 375 mm (15 in) S: 300 mm (1 ft) | July–Sept | Light, acid soil, full sun | Do not feed the plants | Sow thinly from March to May where to flower |
| *Convolvulus tricolor* | Hardy annual. Open bell flowers in pinks and blues | H: 150– 375 mm (6–15 in) S: 230 mm (9 in) | July–Sept | Ordinary, well-drained soil, sunny position | Remove dead flower-heads | Sow where plants are to flower |
| *Dianthus barbatus* Sweet William | Biennial. Many good mixtures in shades of pink, salmon, crimson, and white | H: 450 mm (1½ ft) S: 230 mm (9 in) | June–July | Well-drained preferably alkaline soil, full sun | Good for cutting, colourful and fragrant | Sow outdoors from April to June. Prick off seedlings in nursery rows and set plants in position in Sept–Oct |
| *D. chinensis* 'Heddewigii' Indian or Chinese pink | Half-hardy annual. Brightly-coloured single or double 'pinks'. 'Baby Doll' is one of the best singles | H: 200– 300 mm (8–12 in) S: 150–250 mm (6–10 in) | June–Sept | As *D. barbatus* | Very bright and free-flowering | Sow under glass in Feb–April. Plant out from May onwards |
| *Dimorphotheca* African daisy | Hardy annual. Apricot, orange, primrose and salmon | H: 300 mm (1 ft) S: 230 mm (9 in) | June–Sept | Will grow in poor, dry soil, full sun, shelter | Remove all dead heads to encourage further flowering | Sow outdoors in April–June |
| *Echium plantagineum* Viper's bugloss | Hardy annual. Loose sprays of blue, mauve, pink or white flowers. Dwarf forms preferred | H: 300 mm (1 ft) S: 300 mm (1 ft) | June–Oct | Light soil, open, sunny site | Easy to grow and long-lasting | Sow outdoors in March–May |
| *Eschscholzia californica* Californian poppy | Hardy annual. Brilliant shades of orange, red, yellow, rose, white | H: 300 mm (1 ft) S: 300 mm (1 ft) | June–Oct | Poor soil, full sun | Self-seeds readily | Sow in March–May where it is to flower |

**Above** *Half-hardy annual French marigolds* (Tagetes patula) *come in an array of warm colours, from palest yellow to deepest bronze-red. There are single- and double-flowered varieties and, latest offering from the breeders, Giant Crested forms.*

**Above right** *Rich blue ageratums (this one is* A. houstonianum) *are among the few annual summer-bedding plants that tolerate dry soil and light shade. Use them to make a carpet around the base of trees and large shrubs. Plants raised in early spring and planted out in May can be expected to flower for about five months.*

## Bedding Plants (continued)

| NAME | DESCRIPTION | HEIGHT/ SPREAD | IN FLOWER | SOIL AND SITE | REMARKS | PROPAGATION |
|---|---|---|---|---|---|---|
| *Godetia grandiflora* | Hardy annual. 'Dwarf Bedding Mixed' (H: 300 mm/1 ft, S: 200 mm/8 in) | See description | July–Oct | Light, moist soil, sunny position | Do not feed, as it may encourage lush growth at expense of flowers | Sow in March or April where plants are to flower |
| *Helichrysum bracteatum* Strawflower | Half-hardy annual. Papery 'everlasting' flowers. Good strain is 'Bright Bikini'. H: 300 m/1 ft, S: 230 mm/9 in). | See description | July–Sept | Light, well-drained soil, sunny site | Remove dead flower-heads | Sow under glass in March or April; plant out in May |
| *Iberis umbellata* Candytuft | Hardy annual: Flattish heads of small but bright pink, lavender, purple and white flowers | H: 300 mm (1 ft) S: 300 mm (1 ft) | June–Sept | Ordinary soil, sunny site | Remove dead flower-heads | Sow where plants are to flower from March to May |
| *Impatiens wallerana* Busy-lizzie | Half-hardy perennial grown as an annual. Scarlet, pink, orange and white flower colours. 'Imp' and 'Futura Mixed' are both dependable F1 hybrid mixtures (H: 230 mm/ 9 in; S: 230 mm) | See description | June–Oct | Good garden soil, shade or semi-shade | Useful for difficult shady spots | Sow from Feb to March in a temperature of 15–20°C (60–68°F). Germination is usually slow: Plant out from late May onwards |
| *Linaria maroccana* Toadflax | Hardy annual. Tiny snapdragon flowers in several colour combinations. | H: 230 mm (9 in) S: 150 mm (6 in) | June–July | Ordinary soil, sunny position | Cut plants back after first flush of flower – a second may follow | Sow thinly, where the plants are to flower, from March to May |
| *Lobelia erinus* | Half-hardy annual: Neat, free-flowering annual, frequently planted with alyssum. The compact cultivars (H: 100–150 mm/4–6 in, S: 150 mm/6 in) include 'Cambridge Blue' (pale blue) and 'Crystal Palace' (dark blue, bronze foliage) | See description | May–Oct | Rich, moist soil, sun or part shade | Ensure roots do not become dry | Sow in a heated greenhouse from Jan to March. Prick off seedlings as small clusters. Plant out from late May |

| NAME | DESCRIPTION | HEIGHT/ SPREAD | IN FLOWER | SOIL AND SITE | REMARKS | PROPAGATION |
|---|---|---|---|---|---|---|
| *Lobularia maritima* (syn. *Alyssum maritimum*) | Hardy annual. The most widely known cultivar is the white 'Little Dorrit', but there are carmine-red, violet-pink and deep violet-purple varieties | H: 100 mm (4 in) S: 200 mm (8 in) | June–Oct | Ordinary soil, full sun | Trouble-free plants, easy to grow | Sow where plants are to flower, from March to June. |
| *Myosotis* Forget-me-not | Biennial. Among best cultivars are 'Miniature Blue' (H: 15 cm/6 in, S: 15 cm/6 in) and 'Royal Blue' (H: 30 cm/ 300 mm/12 in, S: 200 mm/8 in) | See description | March–June | Moist soil, partial shade | Keep young plants moist at roots. Self-seeds easily | Sow outdoors from May to July; plant in flowering position in autumn |
| *Nemesia strumosa* | Half-hardy annual. 'Carnival Mixed' is bronze, cerise, crimson, pink, orange, scarlet and yellow | H: 200 mm (8 in) S: 150 mm (6 in) | June–Aug | Ordinary soil, full sun or part shade | Do not allow plants to become dry at roots | Sow from Feb. to May in heated greenhouse. Plant out from late May |
| *Nigella damascena* Love-in-a-mist | Hardy annual. Spidery flowers set amid feathery foliage. 'Miss Jekyll' (H: 450 mm/ 1½ ft, S: 300 mm/1 ft) has cornflower-blue flowers, 'Persian Jewels' (H: 375 mm/15 in, S: 300 mm/1 ft) is mixture of blue, mauve, pink, purple and rosy-red flowers | See description | June–Aug | Any well drained soil, full sun | Remove dead flower-heads to prolong flowering period | Sow where plants are to flower, from March to May for summer flowering, or in Sept for spring flowering |
| *Petunia × hybrida* | Half-hardy annual. Invaluable bedding plants, with masses of bright open trumpet flowers in many colours. Multiflora 'Resisto' types best; Grandiflora forms have larger flowers | H: 300– 375 mm (12–15 in) S: 300 mm (1 ft) | July–Sept | Light, well-rained soil, sheltered position, in full sun | Dead-head regularly | Sow from Feb to March under glass. Plant out in late May. |
| *Tagetes erecta* African marigold | Half-hardy annual. Fine bedding plant with large globular yellow or orange flowers. | H: 250– 300 mm (10–12 in) S: 230 mm (9 in) | June–Oct | Rich soil, sunny site | Remove dead-heads to prolong flowering period | Sow in slightly heated greenhouse in Feb–April; plant out in May–June |
| *T. patula* French marigold | Smaller than African forms. Dwarf single 'Naughty Marietta' (yellow boldly splashed with maroon) and 'Tiger Eyes' (ruffled orange crest within bronze-maroon petals) | H: 150– 250 mm (6–10 in) S: 150 mm (6 in) | June–Oct | Rich soil, sunny site | Very prolific; often flowers while still in seedbox. Hybrids between French and African forms are available | As *T. erecta* |
| *Viola* Pansy, violet, viola | Biennial. Both pansies (cultivars of *V. × wittrockiana*) and violas (cultivars of *V. cornuta*) are short-lived perennials best treated as biennials. Violas have smaller flowers and more upright habit than pansies. Good pansies include 'Majestic Giants' (H, S: 200 mm/ 8 in, mixed) and 'Roggli Swiss Giants' (H: 175 mm/7 in, S: 230 mm/9 in, mixed). Good violas: 'Alba' (H: 230 mm/9 in, S: 300 mm/12 in, white); 'Blue Heaven' (H: 150 mm/6 in, S: 200 mm/8 in, blue) | H: 150– 230 mm (6–9 in) S: 200–300 mm (8–12 in) | April–July | Moist, rich soil, semi-shade | Dead-head regularly | Sow in cold-frame or open ground in June-July; prick out into nursery beds. Move to flowering positions in Sept–Oct |

**Opposite page**
*Combined version of the border plans on pages 24, 29 and 34. Plants could, of course, be less densely packed than here, but the drawing indicates how different sizes and shapes can be exploited to lend structural character to a border.*

### Herbaceous Perennials

| NAME | DESCRIPTION | HEIGHT/ SPREAD | IN FLOWER | SOIL AND SITE | REMARKS | PROPAGATION |
|------|-------------|----------------|-----------|---------------|---------|-------------|
| *Alchemilla mollis* Lady's mantle | Sulphur-yellow flowers carried above rounded leaves | H: 450 mm (1½ ft) S: 300 mm (1 ft) | June–Aug. | Sunny or partly shaded, well-drained soil | Support plants in early stages of growth | Divide between Oct and March |
| *Bergenia cordifolia* Elephant's ears | Large leaves resembling elephants' ears, and sprays of pink flowers | H: 250 mm (10 in) S: 300 mm (1 ft) | April–May | Moist soil, full sun or partial shade | Leave undisturbed unless plants spread excessively | Divide overcrowded plants in March after flowering |
| *Dianthus caryophyllus* Carnation | Parent of many border carnations. Typical cultivars are 'Cherry Clove' (strongly scented, cherry-red); 'Robin Thain' (white flecked crimson) | H: 230 mm (9 in) S: 300 mm (1 ft) | July–Sept | Well-drained limy soil preferred, sunny site | Support with split bamboo canes | Layer stems in July or Aug |
| *Heuchera sanguinea* Alum root, coral bells | Slender stems of tiny bell-shaped, pink or red flowers, carried clear of basal leaves | H: 450 mm (1½ ft) S: 300 mm (1 ft) | June–Sept | Well-drained soil, sun or part shade | Mulch annually. Divide every four years | Lift and divide old plants in Oct or March |
| *Linum narbonnense* Flax | Brilliant blue flowers carried above narrow, grey-green leaves | H: 450 mm (1½ ft) S: 300 mm (1 ft) | June–Sept | Ordinary garden soil in full sun | Plant March–April or Oct. Cut off dead growth in Nov | Take cuttings of soft basal shoots in April |
| *Mertensia virginica* Virginian cowslip | Drooping clusters of purple-blue bells. Foliage dies down in July | H: 450 mm (1½ ft) S: 300 mm (1 ft) | April–June | Moist, rich soil, preferably in partial shade | Lift and replant every three or four years | Divide established plants in Oct or March |
| *Nepeta × faassenii* Catmint | Narrow, grey-green leaves and spikes of lavender flowers. Varieties include 'Blue Beauty' and 'Six Hills Giant' | H: 300–450 mm (1–1½ ft) S: 600 mm (2 ft) | May–Sept | Well-drained soil, sun or partial shade | Cut down plants in autumn | Divide in April. Can also be grown from seed |
| *Physostegia virginiana* 'Vivid' Obedient plant | Rose-lilac tubular flowers carried on stiff stems | H: 600 mm (2 ft) S: 300 mm (1 ft) | Aug–Nov | Ordinary soil, sun or part shade | Water and mulch in dry summer weather | Divide in Oct or April |
| *Polygonum affine* Knotweed | Forms mat of narrow leaves which become coppery in autumn. Pink flowers | H: 150–250 mm (6–10 in) S: 250mm (10in) | June–Sept | Moist fertile soil, sun or part shade | Young plants must not be allowed to become dry at roots | Divide in Oct or April |
| *Sedum spectabile* | Fleshy leaves and flat heads of long-lasting pink or red flowers | H: 300–600 mm (1–2 ft) S: 300–450 mm (1–1½ ft) | Aug–Oct | Ordinary, well-drained soil, full sun | Remove dead flower-heads in spring | Divide established plants in autumn or spring |

**Snapdragon** (Antirrhinum majus) *Half-hardy annual. 'Pumilun' form here is smallest type, good for edging. Flowers June–September. Rich, well-drained soil needed; sunny site. Height 100–150 mm (4–6 in). Sow in January–March.*

**Clarkia pulchella** *Hardy annual. Flowers in mixed colours, double or semi-double, in July–September. Light, slightly acid soil preferred; sunny site. Height 300–450 mm (12–18 in). Sow in March–May.*

**Love-in-a-mist** (Nigella damascena) *Hardy annual. Blue, violet, pink, red or white flowers in June–August, followed by pretty seed pods. Well-drained soil; full sun. Height 150–450 mm (6–18 in). Sow in March.*

**Bergenia cordifolia** *Evergreen perennial.*
*Large, wavy edged leaves. Flowers in*
*March–April. Moist, fertile soil needed; sun*
*or shade. Height 300–450 mm (12–18 in).*
*Divide and replant single-root pieces in*
*autumn.*

**Pot marigold** (Calendula officinalis) *Hardy*
*annual. Large pompom flowers in May–*
*September. Any well-drained soil; bright sun.*
*Height 300–600 mm (1–2 ft). Sow in*
*March–April.*

**Wallflower** (Cheiranthus cheiri) *Biennial.*
*Erect, wiry-stemmed plant. Scented flowers in*
*May–June. Well-drained chalky soil best;*
*full sun. Height 300–600 mm (1–2 ft). Sow*
*in May–June for flowers following year.*

# COLOUR & TEXTURE

Colour is the most obvious part of an ornamental plant's attraction. A dazzling, riotous display of colour from spring to autumn is generally the idea for beginner gardeners. But as time goes on and experience accumulates, this aim gradually changes as you realize that more subtle but more satisfying blendings can be obtained in which colour is mixed with white, or cool greys and silvers, or with plants whose leaves come in a variety of greens.

### HARDY BORDER PLANTS

These are mainly herbaceous plants which 'perform' between April and October, die back in the winter and reappear the following spring. A few have evergreen leaves. Dead heading spent flowers will encourage new buds. Stake the taller varieties.

### ANNUALS & BIENNIALS

Annuals and biennials fill the summer garden and patio with bold and brilliant blocks of colour. Following are easily grown from seed. Annuals flower the year they are planted, biennials the following year. Follow instructions on the seed packet for sowing depth.

### BULBS

Bulbs take up little space and will give colour in the garden almost all year round. Most appreciate a well-cultivated soil and look better planted in clumps or drifts. Allow the leaves of narcissi to die back naturally to encourage healthy growth and flowering the following year.

### QUICK COLOUR

When you are planning for quick colour remember that a small plot in a one-colour theme looks larger and better planned that a hotch-potch, so it is best to stick to pinks with blues or oranges with reds for a more co-ordinated look. On the other hand, if you are creating a 'cottage-garden look', you can use a wide variety of colours.

Many popular annuals come in several different forms. Half-hardy African marigolds (*Tagetes erecta*) make a patch of instant sunshine with their large, orange, pompon heads and range from dwarf to giant forms.

Cornflowers (*Centaurea*) are usually seen in bright blue but also come in pinks and whites; and love-in-a-mist (*Nigella*) can be found in pink and white as well as the usual dark mauve-blue. There are all sorts of new varieties of low-growing nasturtiums (*Tropaeolum majus*), some of them with double blooms. Look for the compact 'Jewel Mixed' if you do not want the plants to spread too far.

*'Orange King' is the finest form of* Berberis linearifolia, *a prickly shrub whose flowers unfold in April. It has a leggy, upright habit, so is best sited behind a round, spreading shrub.*

# ORANGE

Hot and fiery orange is an exciting, vibrant colour, but use it sparingly or it will scream at you. It blends with yellow and should be interplanted with white-flowered plants to relieve the intensity. Orange, together with red, are assertive colours and a small small space can be made to look larger by planting flowers of this hue in the foreground, with blues at the farther end of the garden.

Some of the most striking border plants with flowers in this colour are day lily (*Hemerocallis* 'Fandango'), lighting up summer from June to August; shrubby cinquefoil (*Potentilla fruticosa* 'Tangerine'), a shrub spreading to 600 mm (2 ft) that flowers from May to November; *Berberis linearifolia*. 'Orange King', a robust shrub that grows about 1.8 m (6 ft) high, but is a little on the upright, gaunt side, so is best positioned in a corner; and deciduous azaleas, specially 'Gibraltar', 'Gloria Mundi' 'Peter Koster', and 'Klondyke'. These look superb in front of a deep green hedge or clumps of evergreens such as *Cotoneaster lacteus* and Mexican orange blossom (*Choisya ternata*).

Other dashes of orange are contributed by *Crocosmia* × *crocosmiiflora* 'Emily MacKenzie', whose glowing heads of bloom are borne from July to September among sheaves of sword-shaped leaves. The euphorbias also have an orange-flowered member in the form of *E. griffithii* 'Fireglow', at its most colourful from May to June. Gaillardias with their bright, daisy blooms from June to September are vital to the summer beauty of an herbaceous border and orange-flame *G. grandiflora* 'Mandarin' associates well with the scarlet of red-hot pokers (*Kniphofia*).

Orange is also well represented among the

bedding plants, particularly by the marigolds. Specially fine are the African varieties (*Tagetes erecta*), such as 'Superjack Orange', large flowers on 600 mm (2 ft) stems, 'Inca Orange', and 'Gay Ladies'. The French dwarf doubles (*T. patula*) include 'Orange Boy', a beauty for edging, growing just 150 mm (6 in) high.

Lilies, enjoying light woodland shade and, ideally, the presence of small shrubs such as azaleas growing among them, are a delight. Or you can grow them in deep tubs. Orange-flowered varieties include 'Prince Constantine', with outward-facing petals, that blooms from June to July; and 'Mrs R. O. Backhouse', which also flowers then and is remarkable for producing up to 30 beautiful blooms on a strong pyramidal stem.

*Subtle hints of green and orange in the 'Fireglow' variety of spurge (Euphorbia griffithii) make it a favourite for the flower arranger's border.*

**Shrubby cinquefoil** (Potentilla fruticosa) *Orange variety 'Tangerine' flowers in May–August. Well-drained soil; sunny site. Height 450–600 mm (18–24 in). Take cuttings in autumn.*

**Blanket-flower** (Gaillardia grandiflora 'Mandarin') *Perennial. Flowers in June–October. Likes well-drained soil; sun or light shade. Height 600–900 mm (2–3 ft). Sow February–March.*

**African marigold** (Tagetes erecta 'Inca Orange'). *Dwarf form of half-hardy annual. Flowers in July–October. Well-worked soil; sunny open site. Height 200–250 in (8–10 in). Sow in March–April.*

## YELLOW

We are lucky with yellows: Not only is there a vast choice of flowers in that colour, but there are many gold-leaved and gold or yellow variegated evergreens, too. A yellow border can be warmed by adding a touch of orange or cooled by introducing blue. White-flowered 'dot' plants relieve the intensity. An effective contrast is obtained by interplanting with purple flowers or shrubs, such as the purple-leaved smoke bush (*Cotinus coggygria* 'Royal Purple'). Some yellow-flowered shrubs are happy in shade, and the free-flowering *Forsythia* × *intermedia* 'Lynwood', a blaze of gold in early spring, will brighten a gloomy corner. So will a planting of winter aconites, specially the larger flowered *Eranthis* 'Guinea Gold', and all kinds of daffodils, including the diminutive *Narcissus cyclamineus*, a little charmer whose tiny trumpet blooms rise from a crown of swept-back petals.

The yarrow makes a stately subject for the middle or back of a border. Try *Achillea filipendulina* 'Gold Plate'; growing to 1.2–1.5 m (4–5 ft), its broad flower-heads not only colour the garden from July to August, but can then be cut and dried for winter decoration. It looks superb in association with the taller blue delphiniums.

Other border plants valued for their cheering yellow hues are the deep-yellow tickseed *Coreopsis grandiflora* 'Goldfink', in bloom from summer to autumn; *Kniphofia* 'Yellow Hammer'; leopard's bane (*Doronicum plantagineum* 'Spring Beauty'), prized for its neat, edging habit and double golden flowers; and *Oenothera missouriensis*, a flamboyant trailing form with massive cup-shaped flowers from June to August.

Among bedding plants, *Erysimum* 'Golden Gem', an alpine wallflower for rock gardens, makes a vivid splash in early spring. As for *Gazania* 'Mini-Star Yellow', its bright, starry, daisy flowers shine up at us all summer long. There are also the rich yellow French or African marigolds (*Tagetes*) and the carpeting poached-egg plant (*Limnanthes douglasii*), whose profusion of blooms are white with rich butter-yellow centres.

*Cheering spring with its golden daisy flowers, leopard's-bane* (Doronicum plantagineum) *has a double-flowered form called 'Spring Beauty'. Both thrive in cold, draughty places so are excellent candidates for the more gloomy border.*

*Forsythia × intermedia Deciduous shrub hybrid. Flowers in March–April, before foliage. Free-draining fertile soil, sun or shade. Height 1.8–2.4 m (6–8 ft). Plant October–March.*

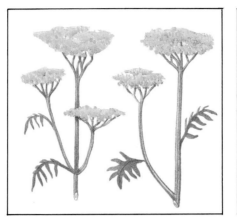

**Yarrow** (Achillea filipendulina *'Gold Plate'*) *Hardy perennial. Flowers in June–September. Well-drained soil; sunny site. Height 900 mm–1.5 m (3–5 ft). Sow in March.*

**Tickseed** (Coreopsis grandiflora *'Goldfink'*) *Perennial. Flowers in June–September. Fertile, well-drained, chalky soil preferred; full sun. Height 600–900 mm (2–3 ft). Take offsets in July–August.*

## SHRUBS
### YELLOW OR ORANGE FLOWERS

| NAME AND HEIGHT | FLOWERS | SITE | NOTES |
|---|---|---|---|
| *Kerria japonica* (jew's mallow) 1.5 m (5 ft) | April–May | Shade | Any soil; easy to grow |
| *Mahonia japonica* to 1.5 m (5 ft) | Jan–March | Shade | Needs space; best at back of border |
| *Potentilla fruticosa* **'Tangerine'** (cinquefoil) 600 mm (2 ft) | May–Nov | Sun or part shade | Many varieties; produces best colour in light shade |
| *Ruta graveolens* **'Jackman's Blue'** (rue) 600 mm (2 ft) | July | Sun or part shade | Dense rounded shape; blue-grey leaf. Clip to keep shape |
| *Senecio ×* **'Sunshine'** 1 m (3¼ ft) | June | Sun | Silver-grey leaves. Spreading. |

## HARDY BORDER PLANTS
### YELLOW FLOWERS

| NAME AND HEIGHT | IN FLOWER | SITE | REMARKS |
|---|---|---|---|
| *Achillea ×* **'Moonshine'** (yarrow) 600 mm (2 ft) | June–Aug | Full sun | Silvery foliage |
| *Alchemilla mollis* (lady's mantle) 450 mm (1½ ft) | June–July | Sun or part shade | Pretty leaf; good for ground cover |
| *Coreopsis verticillata* (tickseed) 600 mm (2 ft) | June–Sept | Sun | Good for cutting |
| *Epimedium perralderianum* (barrenwort) 300 mm (1 ft) | April–May | Part or full shade | Ground cover; needs cool moist soil |
| *Euphorbia polychroma* (spurge) 450 mm (1½ ft) | April–May | Sun or part shade | Mound-forming |
| *Hemerocallis* (day lily) 450 mm (1½ ft) | June–Aug | Sun or shade | Needs moist soil. Plant in clumps |
| *Solidago* **'Caesia'** (golden rod) 900 m (3 ft) | Sept–Oct | Sun or part shade | Good for back of border |
| *Verbascum ×* **'Gainsborough'** 1.2 m (4 ft) | July–Aug | Sun | Good on chalk. Felty leaves |

### ORANGE FLOWERS

| NAME AND HEIGHT | FLOWERS | SITE | NOTES |
|---|---|---|---|
| *Alstroemeria aurantiaca* (Peruvian lily) 600 mm (2 ft) | June | Full sun | Rich soil |
| *Crocosmia masonorum* **'Firebird'** 750 mm (2½ ft) | July–Aug | Full sun | Lovely by paths or front of border |
| *Kniphofia* **'Ada'** (red-hot poker) 450 mm (1½ ft) | Sept–Oct | Sun | Moist, well-drained soil |

## ANNUALS & BIENNIALS
### YELLOW/ORANGE FLOWERS

| NAME | SOW | FLOWERS | HEIGHT | NOTES |
|---|---|---|---|---|
| *Calendula* (A) (pot marigold) | March–May | May–Aug | 300 mm (1 ft) | Sun or part shade |
| *Cheiranthus* (B) (wallflower) | June | May–June | 300 mm (1 ft) | Sun or part shade |
| *Cosmos* (A) (cosmea) | April–May | July–Sept | 900 m (3 ft) | Sun or part shade |
| *Tagetes patula* (A) (French marigold) | April–May | July–Oct | 150 mm (6 in) | Sun |

## BULBS
### YELLOW/ORANGE FLOWERS

| NAME AND HEIGHT | PLANT | FLOWERS | NOTES |
|---|---|---|---|
| *Crocus ancyrensis* **'Golden Bunch'** 100 mm (4 in) | Sept–Oct | Dec–Jan | Well-drained soil, full sun |
| *Eranthis hyemalis* (winter aconite) 50 mm (2 in) | Aug–Sept | Jan–Feb | Moist soil |
| *Narcissus* (daffodil) to 450 mm (18 in) | Sept | March–April | Full sun. Many varieties |

## RED

When planning a red scheme, combine it with coppery-leaved plants, such as the purple-leaved cobnut (*Corylus maxima* 'Purpurea'), cutting the shrub back to a stump each winter to encourage a display of extra-large leaves. Or set red-flowered plants against a coppiced Pissard's purple plum (*Prunus pissardii*).

There are a few reds to choose from early in the year, and we rely on tulips, specially the *Tulipa greigii* hybrids, such as scarlet 'Red Riding Hood', and the *T. kaufmanniana* beauties renowned for their big blooms.

As spring advances the rock rose (*Helianthemum*) makes a carpet of bloom, and scarlet 'Red Dragon' and 'Mrs C. W. Earle' light up sunny patches. They have a sprawling, creeping habit, so arrange them on banks or use them to clothe rock-garden outcrops where their charm can be seen to advantage.

In summer, the field widens. Crocosmias, day lilies (*Hemerocallis*) and roses make their debut. Break up these zones of scarlet with arching, green-leaved grasses. Most striking of these are the feathery plumed *Pennisetum alopecuroides* and *Stipa pennata* (feather grass). Scarlet combines beautifully with white and a bed of floribunda roses: brilliant red 'Evelyn Fison', for instance, looks magnificent if interplanted with 'Iceberg', the purest white.

Another exciting contrast is achieved when scarlet-flowered *Crocosmia* 'Lucifer' or 'Vulcan' is planted close to the golden-leaved black-locust tree, *Robina pseudoacacia* 'Frisia'.

There are many contenders for this colour in bedding plants, too, and a tub or trough of *Pelargonium* 'Cherry Diamond' or 'Red Elite' positioned against a white wall hints of the Mediterranean.

**Tulip** (T. greigii *'Red Riding Hood'*) *Bulb. Flowers in April. Leaves characteristically marbled. Fertile, well-drained soil; full sun. Height 300 mm (1 ft). Plant bulbs in mid-autumn.*

**Rock rose** (Helianthemum *'Red Dragon'*) *Evergreen dwarf shrub. Flowers in May– July on trailing shoots. Likes chalky, well-drained soil; full sun. Height 250 mm (10 in). Take soft cuttings in June–July.*

**Pelargonium 'Cherry Diamond'** *Tender perennial. Flowers in summer, two to three weeks earlier than other seed-raised varieties. Well-drained soil; full sun. Height 300 mm (1 ft). Take soft cuttings in March–April.*

*Hydrangea 'Europa' Shrub. Mophead (Hortensia) variety; flowers in July–September. Flowers blue in acid soils. Fertile soil; sheltered site, part shaded. Height 1.2–1.8 m (4–6 ft). Take cuttings in summer.*

*Rose 'Louise Odier' Richly scented, blooms throughout summer. Well-drained, moisture-retentive soil; open, sunny site. Height 1.5 m (5 ft). Take ripe-wood cuttings in September–November.*

*Mallow (Lavatera trimestris 'Silver Cup') Hardy annual. Flowers continuously in July–October. Well-drained soil, chalk tolerated; bright sun. Height 1–1.2 m (3¼–4 ft). Sow in April or September.*

## PINK

Tranquil and accommodating, pink is an 'easy' colour and there is a wide range of plants that provide it. Associating naturally with white, blending with red, and contrasing effectively with yellow, it reflects light well. Pink-flowered plants should be set against a dark, green background, such as a holly or yew hedge, or clumps of white-flowered hostas.

Pink looks well in tubs. Hydrangeas, such as 'Europa' and 'Holstein' (mophead kinds that bloom in late summer), stay compact and free-flowering when their roots are confined.

Among roses, coppery-pink 'Albertine', a robust rambler flowering in midsummer, makes a colourful backcloth and is ideal for clothing a chain-link fence or section of trellis. The floribunda 'Dearest', in salmon-pink, has a vigorous nature, grows about 750 mm (2½ ft) high, and looks well flanking a path or drive. The Bourbon roses are also well represented (with the bonus that most are sweetly scented). Finest are rich pink 'La Reine Victoria', whose exquisite cupped blooms are set against light green foliage; 'Kathleen Harrop', a beautiful shell-pink form of the bright carmine 'Zéphirine Drouhin'; and, most glorious of all, 'Louise Odier', deep rose-pink, and robust. All these flower in midsummer.

Border perennials with pink blooms include hybrids of the Peruvian lily (*Alstroemeria ligtu*), a sun-lover for a warm, wind-free border. In early summer, it becomes a mass of blooms.

Brightening spring and early summer are oriental poppies (*Papaver orientale*), especially 'Mrs Perry', which is pink with dark blotches, and the peonies, whose beautiful pink forms include 'Edulis Superba' and rose-scented 'Lady Alexandra Duff'.

Summer bedding annuals can be found in many pink shades: the corn-cockle (*Agrostemma githago* 'Milas') has large pink flowers and makes an impressive clump in the middle of a border; *Cosmea* 'Sensation Mixed' contains many powder-pink hues and it flowers for many weeks in summer; and lovely mallow *Lavatera trimestris* 'Silver Cup', with silver-pink blooms.

**Opposite page, top**
*Day lily (Hemerocallis 'Burning Daylight'), with its large, richly coloured flowers, blooms in mid-summer.*

## SHRUBS

| NAME AND HEIGHT | FLOWERS | SITE | NOTES |
|---|---|---|---|
| **PINK OR RED FLOWERS** | | | |
| *Kolkwitzia amabilis* 'Pink Cloud' (beauty bush) 1.5 m (5 ft) | May–June | Sun or part shade | Broad and twiggy; free-flowering |
| *Ribes sanguineum* 'Pulborough Scarlet' (flowering currant) 2 m (6½ ft) | April–May | Shade | Upright; fast grower; good for quick effort |
| *Viburnum fragrans* 2 m (6½ ft) | Nov–Feb | Sun or part shade | Slender, upright. Winter flowering |

## HARDY BORDER PLANTS
### RED FLOWERS

| NAME AND HEIGHT | FLOWERS | SITE | NOTES |
|---|---|---|---|
| *Aquilegia* 'Crimson Star' (columbine) 600 mm (2 ft) | May–June | Sun or part shade | Needs moisture |
| *Aster novi-belgii* 'Carnival' (Michaelmas daisy) 900 mm (3 ft) | Sept–Oct | Sun or part shade | Good for back of border |
| *Lychnis chalcedonica* (campion) 900 mm–1.2 m (3–4 ft) | June–July | Sun | Good for back of border |
| *Stachys olympica* (lamb's tongue) 300 mm (1 ft) | June–Aug | Sun or shade | Good for ground cover. Silver felty leaf |

## HARDY BORDER PLANTS

### PINK FLOWERS

| NAME AND HEIGHT | IN FLOWER | SITE | NOTES |
|---|---|---|---|
| Anemone × hybrida 600 mm (2 ft) | Aug–Oct | Sun or shade | Late-flowering |
| Lamium maculatum 'Chequers' (dead-nettle) 300 mm (1 ft) | May | Shade | Marbled leaf. Good ground cover under trees. |
| Paeonia 'Lady Alexander Duff' (peony) 750 mm (2½ ft) | June | Sun | Deep rich soil. Leave undisturbed |
| Phlox paniculata 'Balmoral' 600 mm (2 ft) | June | Part shade | Light, moist soil |

## ANNUALS & BIENNIALS
### PINK/RED FLOWERS

| NAME | SOW | FLOWERS | HEIGHT | SITE |
|---|---|---|---|---|
| Clarkia (A) | March–April | July–Aug | 300 mm (1 ft) | Sun |
| Digitalis (B) (foxglove) | July | June–July | 1.2–1.5 (4–5 ft) | Part shade |
| Godetia grandiflora 'Sybil Sherwood' (A) | March–April | July–Aug | 300 mm (1 ft) | Sun or part shade |
| Linum (A) (flax) | March–April | July–Aug | 450 mm (1½ ft) | Sun or part shade |
| Lavatera (A) (mallow) | April | July–Sept | 900 mm (3 ft) | Sun or part shade |
| Tropaeolum majus (A) (nasturtium) | April–May | July–Sept | 300 mm (1 ft) | Sun or part shade |
| Papaver (A) (poppy) | March–April | June–Sept | 750 mm (2½ ft) | Sun or part shade |
| Phlox drummondii (A) | March–April | July–Oct | 150 mm (6 in) | Sun or part shade |

## BULBS
### PINK/RED FLOWERS

| NAME | SOW | FLOWERS | NOTES |
|---|---|---|---|
| Amaryllis belladonna 450 mm (18 in) | Aug–Sept | Aug–Oct | Needs warm south-facing wall, moist, well-drained soil |
| Cyclamen neapolitanum 100 mm (4 in) | Sept–Oct | Aug–Nov | Partial or full shade. Good under trees |
| Tulipa 250–450 mm (10–18 in) | Nov | March–April | Well-drained soil in full sun. |

**Right** *Brightening rock-garden pockets, window-boxes and tubs in February and March, crocuses repay generous planting. Here 'Warley Rose', a fine purple cultivar of C. chrysanthus, blends nicely with white and yellow varieties.*

**Right** *Dead-nettle (Lamium maculatum) adds a touch of floral pink to its ground-cover role, for which its attractive silver-splashed leaves are a boon. Rather aggressive, the plant may need to be curbed in smaller borders.*

## BLUE

An open, sunny situation is best for blue flowers: in light shade they absorb light and are difficult to see. Delphiniums, meconopsis and gentians contribute the purest blues, and generous beds of them, if possible backed with green-leaved shrubs or the tall, arching leaves of grasses and day lilies, can make a wonderfully relaxing show.

Blue associates pleasingly with yellow or white, and also with its close relatives in the spectrum – mauve, lavender, purple and violet.

Blue-flowered bulbs aplenty brighten early spring. Two of the most reliable are lobelia-blue *Crocus chrysanthus* 'Blue Pearl' and flax-blue grape hyacinth, *Muscari armeniacum* 'Blue Spire'.

Among shrubs, *Hydrangea serrata* 'Bluebird', a lace-cap type, and its mophead cousin *H. macrophylla* 'Générale Vicomtesse de Vibraye', colour to a deep ultramarine-blue on acid soil. If your soil is neutral or limy, you can induce a colour change by treating the root area with a hydrangea colourant sold at garden centres, or by burying pieces of iron among the roots. Two late summer/early autumn flowering shrubs valued for their attractive blue flowers are the blue spiraea (*Caryopteris* 'Ferndown') and *Hibiscus* 'Blue Bird'.

Summer would not be the same without a clump or two of rich blue African lilies, notably *Agapanthus* 'Headbourne Hybrids', which are ideal for borders or for tubs to enhance the patio. Among annuals, the glorious *Salvia farinacea* 'Victoria' looks superb when interplanted with ferny-leaved sea ragwort (*Senecio cineraria*), of which 'Silver Dust' is a fine dwarf form.

Of blue-related colours, purple (like red and orange) is an extravagant colour and should be used in moderation – for instance, in small patches, or at the far end of the garden, or in combination with yellow, where its richness won't appear to foreshorten the view. Among the most striking purple-flowered border perennials are *Salvia nemorosa* 'Superba', a mass of fetching spikes up to 1 m (3 ft) tall; *Delphinium*

'King Arthur', to 1.8 m (6 ft); and the purple cone-flower, *Echinacea purpurea*, to 1.8 m (6 ft). These light up the border in summer.

Violet-purple can be found in the 'Hidcote' variety of lavender, which grows some 600 mm (2 ft) high, and that choice little edger, lily turf (*Liriope muscari*), especially the cultivar 'Majestic', whose dense racemes of rounded flowers bloom in autumn.

**Below** *'Hidcote' is one of the best of the compact forms of old English lavender* (Lavandula angustifolia). *Richly scented, its purple flowers attract butterflies.*

# SHRUBS

| NAME AND HEIGHT | PLANT | SITE | NOTES |
|---|---|---|---|
| **BLUE FLOWERS** | | | |
| *Ceanothus* × **'Cascade'** (Californian lilac) 1.2 m (4 ft) | May–June | Sun | Best against sunny wall; spreading habit |
| *Hibiscus syriacus* **'Bluebird'** 2.1 m (7 ft) | Aug–Sept | Sun | Sheltered position, well-drained soil |
| *Lavandula spica* **'Hidcote'** (lavender) 300 mm (1 ft) | July–Sept | Sun | Well-drained light soil. Trim in April and August |

# HARDY BORDER PLANTS
## BLUE FLOWERS

| | PLANT | SITE | NOTES |
|---|---|---|---|
| *Ajuga reptans* (bugle) 150 mm (6 in) | May–June | Sun or part shade | Good for ground cover. Bronze leaf |
| *Brunnera macrophylla* 450 mm (1½ ft) | May–June | Sun or shade | Ground cover |
| *Campanula persicifolia* (bellflower) 900 mm (3 ft) | June–Aug | Sun or part shade | Needs moisture |
| *Geranium* (*grandiflorum*) (crane's-bill) 300 mm (1 ft) | May–June | Sun or part shade | Ground cover |

**Willow gentian** (Gentiana asclepiadea) *Perennial. Flowers in July–September. Likes damp soil; prefers a cool, shady, moist site. Height 400–600 mm (16–24 in). Sow in summer.*

*Hibiscus syriacus* **'Blue Bird'** *Hardy deciduous shrub. Large-toothed leaves. Flowers in August–October. Well-drained, fertile soil; full sun, open site. Height and spread 1.8 m (6 ft). Take cuttings in July.*

*Salvia farinacea* **'Victoria'** *Half-hardy annual. Intense blue flowers in June–July. Fairly rich, free-draining soil; open, sunny site. Height 450 mm (1½ ft). Sow in March–April.*

## ANNUALS & BIENNIALS
### BLUE FLOWERS

| NAME | SOW | FLOWERS | HEIGHT | NOTES |
|---|---|---|---|---|
| Centaurea cyanus (A) (cornflower) | March–April | June–Sept | 600 mm (2 ft) | Sun or part shade |
| Delphinium chinensis (A) | Sept | June–Sept | 450 mm (1½ ft) | Sun or part shade |
| Echium plantagineum (A) (viper's bugloss) | March–April | July–Aug | 300 mm (1 ft) 230 mm (9 in) | Sun or part shade |
| Lobelia erinus (A) | Feb–March | May–Oct | | Sun or part shade |
| Myosotis sylvatica (B) (forget-me-not) | June–July | April-May | 150 mm (6 in) | Sun or part shade |
| Nemesia (A) | May | July–Sept | 300 mm (1 ft) | Sun or part shade |
| Nigella damascena (A) (love-in-a-mist) | March–April | June–Aug | 230 mm (9 in) | Sun or part shade |

## BULBS
### BLUE FLOWERS

| NAME AND HEIGHT | PLANT | FLOWERS | NOTES |
|---|---|---|---|
| Chionodoxa (glory-of-the-snow) 150 mm (6 in) | Oct | Feb–March | Well-drained soil in full sun |
| Hyacinthus orientalis 300 mm (1 ft) | Oct | March–April | As above |
| Muscari armeniacum (grape hyacinth) 200 mm (8 in) | Sept–Oct | March–May | Full sun |
| Scilla sibirica (squill) 150 mm (6 in) | Oct | Feb–March | Moist, well-drained soil, part shade |

### PURPLE FLOWERS

| | | | |
|---|---|---|---|
| Erythronium denscanis (dog's-tooth violet) 150 mm (6 in) | Sept | March–April | Moist soil; part shade |
| Fritillaria meleagris | Sept–Nov | April–June | Moist soil. Looks best in rough grass. |

## WHITE & GREEN

White is indispensable: we use it to break up and tone down fierce orange, red and yellow flowers; to create a cool, single colour bed or border; to lighten a gloomy spot. The famous white border at Sissinghurst Castle (Kent) cleverly interposes silver- and grey-leaved plants between the flowers and the backing green-leaved hedge.

There is a tremendous choice of 'whites' and, by careful selection, it is often better to choose creamy rather than the starched 'white' forms as the former are more restful on the eye. There are white forms of most border plants – delphinium, campanula, dianthus, chrysanthemum, armeria, aster, kniphofia, iris and many others. Shrubs with white flowers are well represented, with magnolia, deutzia, philadelphus and viburnum.

Creamy white roses are a joy – but finding varieties resistant to black spot and other diseases can be difficult. Happily, the hybrid musks seldom let you down, and white-flushed lemon 'Moonlight' is sweetly scented.

There are plenty of white-flowered annuals. Pick from *Ageratum* 'Spindrift', *Alyssum* 'Snowdrift', *Arctotis grandis*, candytuft *Iberis* 'White Spiral', and *Dianthus heddewigii* 'Snow Fire'.

Among bulbs we are spoilt for choice, with white-flowered tulip, narcissus, crocus, grape hyacinth (*Muscari*), hyacinth, and anemone.

Green-flowered plants have special charm and are best used on their own. Favourites among them are winter-flowering hellebore (*Helleborus foetidus*) and its spring-flowering cousin (*H. corsicus*). The euphorbias are a delight, too, with *E. robbiae's* pea-green blooms enriching light shade in early spring. A plant popular with flower arrangers is the 'Lime Green' variety of the sweet-scented tobacco plant, *Nicotiana alata*. A bedding plant with a difference is bells-of-Ireland (*Moluccella laevis*), which is prized by flower arrangers for winter displays.

## SHRUBS

| NAME AND HEIGHT | PLANT | SITE | NOTES |
|---|---|---|---|
| **WHITE FLOWERS** | | | |
| Magnolia stellata 900 mm (3 ft) | March–April | Sun | Needs sheltered site. |
| Philadelphus 'Sybille' (mock-orange) 1.2 m (4 ft) | June–July | Sun or part shade | Fragrant flowers marked with purple |
| Pieris 'Forest Flame' 1.5 m (5 ft) | May | Shade | Lime-hater; needs sheltered site |
| Pyracantha rogersiana (firethorn) 2.1 m (7 ft) | June | Sun or shade | Good for dark walls. Scarlet berries |
| Spiraea thunbergii 300 mm (1 ft) | March–April | Sun or part shade | Small and twiggy. Free-flowering |

**Giant bellflower** (Campanula latifolia) *Perennial. Flowers 65 mm (2½ in) long in July. Likes well-drained, chalky soil; sun or light shade. Height 1.2 m (4 ft). Sow in March–April.*

*Iris germanica* **'Cliffs of Dover'.** *German or bearded type; perennial. Flowers in May–June. Free-draining soil, must be alkaline; open, sunny site. Height 1 m (3 ft). Plant after flowering.*

**Spurge** (Euphorbia robbiae) *Evergreen perennial. Flowers in March–June. Light, peaty soil; tolerates some shade. Height 450–600 mm (1½–2 ft). Root basal cuttings in spring and autumn.*

**Tobacco plant** (Nicotiana alata 'Lime Green') *Half-hardy annual. Scented flowers in June–October. Well-drained soil; sun or partial shade. Height 600 mm–1.2 m (2–4 ft). Sow in March.*

There are also green-flowered tulips and 'Angel', a Double Early Viridiflora variety, is yellowish white with apple-green petals.

## HARDY BORDER PLANTS

| NAME AND HEIGHT | FLOWERS | SITE | NOTES |
|---|---|---|---|
| **WHITE FLOWERS** | | | |
| *Convallaria majalis* (lily-of-the-valley) 200 mm (8 in) | April–May | Part shade | Good for ground cover. Fragrant. Needs moisture |
| *Helleborus niger* (Christmas rose) 300 mm (1 ft) | Jan–March | Shade | Needs moist rich loam. Feed with manure in spring |
| *Dianthus plumarius* 'Mrs Sinkins' (pink) 300 mm (1 ft) | June–July | Sun | Needs well-drained soil |

## BULBS
### WHITE FLOWERS

| NAME AND HEIGHT | PLANT | FLOWERS | NOTES |
|---|---|---|---|
| *Colchicum autumnale* 'Album' (autumn crocus) 230 mm (9 in) | July | Sept | Full sun or light shade |
| *Galanthus nivalis* (snowdrop) 150 mm (6 in) | July–Aug | Jan | In grass or among shrubs |
| *Leucojum vernum* (snowflake) 450 mm (18 in) | Oct | April–May | Moist soil; part shade |
| *Ornithogalum nutans* (drooping star of Bethlehem) 250–350 mm (10–14 in) | March–April | June | Sun or part shade |

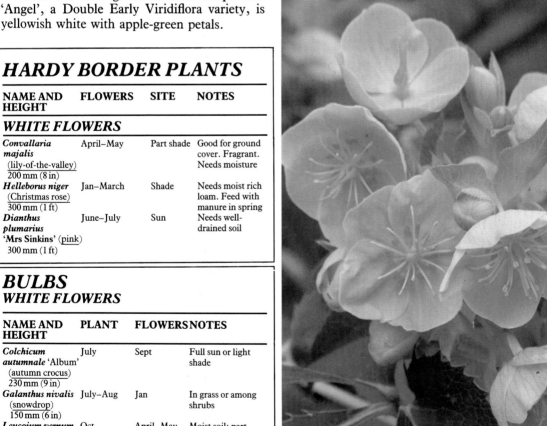

## FOLIAGE COLOURS

Coloured foliage – golden-yellow, copper, purple, red, silver and variegated – is a boon. Shrubs, border plants, annuals and climbers that possess it enrich the garden as much as colourful flowers.

If you are looking through the catalogues, cultivars called 'Aurea', 'Aureum' or 'Aureus' indicate that their leaves are golden (from Latin *aureus*, golden).

One of the finest is the full-moon maple, *Acer japonicum* 'Aureum'. This elegant, slow-growing tree is somewhat wind-frost-tender, so site it in a sheltered spot. *Berberis thunbergii* 'Aurea' almost dazzles with the intensity of its butter-yellow leaves. It makes a smallish bush and is best positioned well away from more robust shrubs that could smother it. Out of the sun, its leaves turn green, so keep it in an open site.

Heathers provide us with 'Gold Feather', 'Gold Haze' and 'Joy Vanstone' forms of *Calluna vulgaris*, commonly called ling. Though these flower in late summer, the beauty of their leaves is best appreciated in winter.

Golden privet (*Ligustrum ovalifolium* 'Aureum') is a neat shrub and good for hedging. If green-leaved shoots appear, cut them out to prevent them from dominating. One of the few golden-leaved shrubs to retain its colour in light shade is the mock orange, *Philadelphus coronarius* 'Aureus'. Cut this back each spring to enjoy a robust regrowth of handsome stems clad with extra large leaves. Another golden beauty is the elderberry, *Sambucus racemosa* 'Plumosa'. This must have a sunny spot or the gold will pale to green.

*A dazzling display of primrose-yellow foliage is your reward for planting the 'Aureum' variety of the full-moon maple (*Acer japonicum*). Slow-growing and compact, it is ideal for the smaller garden. Plant in deep, rich, peaty soil in a site sheltered from icy winds.*

**Left** *One of the most strikingly coloured barberries, B. thunbergii 'Rose Glow' looks splendid on its own or associated with its golden-leaved cousin 'Aurea'. As a hedge, it stays low, about 600 mm (2 ft), and is easily trimmed.*

Two spectacular border perennials are *Valeriana phu* 'Aurea' and *Hosta fortunei* 'Aurea'. Both start life a brilliant golden yellow, commanding attention until mid-summer, when the leaves pale to lime-green.

Purple-leaved plants are indicated by the words 'Purpurea' or 'Purpureum' (from the old English for heraldic purple). A choice shrub for a tub or gap in the paving stones on a terrace or patio is the Japanese maple, *Acer palmatum* 'Dissectum Atropurpureum'. It grows very slowly and its intriguing umbrella habit draws admiring comments. A really first-class shrub is *Berberis* × *ottowensis* 'Purpurea' (syn. 'Superba'), whose yellow flowers and red berries complement the vinous purple of its leaves. Its cousin, *B. thunbergii* 'Atropurea Nana' (syn. 'Little Favourite'), makes a splendid feature for a rock garden.

Others to look out for – and remember, they make a perfect backcloth for red-flowered plants – are the filbert *Corylus maxima* 'Purpurea', smoke tree *Cotinus coggygria* 'Royal Purple', and blackthorn *Prunus spinosa* 'Purpurea'.

Cream or yellow variegated plants, mostly shrubs, are very appealing, and evergreens among them become a focus in winter. *Elaeagnus pungens* 'Maculata' is prized for its evergreen leaves which are brightened by a central splash of gold. *E.* × *ebbingei* 'Gilt Edge' is one of a number of varieties with green leaves fetchingly rimmed with gold.

*Euonymus fortunei radicans* 'Silver Queen's leaves are edged in creamy white, but in early spring the young leaves open a creamy yellow colour with a pale border. *E. japonicus* 'Ovatus Aureus', a cultivar of a popular hedging shrub for coastal gardens, has very attractive golden yellow variegation. *Hebe* × *franciscana* 'Variegata' is slightly less hardy than the hybrid type, but it will flourish in a sheltered corner, producing its creamy variegated leaves all year.

Among the hollies (Ilex), there are two excellent clones of *I. aquifolium*: the broad-leaved common form 'Argenteo-marginata' (silver variegation) and 'Golden Queen' (deep yellow). The pittosporums include some of the most beautiful evergreen shrubs; unfortunately, most of them are too tender to thrive outdoors in this country. Hardier than most is *P. tenuifolium*, which is well worth trying if you live in a warmer part of the south or west. Two cultivars with variegation are 'Silver Queen' (silvery white) and 'Variegatum' (creamy white). In both, the colours contrast strikingly with the black stems. *Weigela florida* is a very popular medium-sized shrub bearing pink, bell-shaped flowers in May and June. Its cultivar 'Variegata' has cream-edged leaves.

**Below** *Of all weigelas, W. florida 'Variegata' is most suitable in a shrub or mixed border for breaking up hotter colours – reds, yellows and oranges. Its arching branches are decked with bloom from May to June and its creamy-yellow-rimmed leaves stay bright all summer. (For its non-variegated parent, see page 6.)*

## COLOUR CHANGES

We all delight in the turn of green leaves of deciduous trees to glorious browns and golds in the autumn. One of the most interesting recent developments has been the introduction of evergreen shrub cultivars whose leaves change colour from season to season. The most striking of these are clones of *Calluna vulgaris*, the common heather of the English and Scottish countryside. Among the finest of these clones are 'Blazeaway', which is green in summer and rich red in winter; 'Golden Feather', light gold in summer, deeper gold in winter; 'Gold Haze', a 600 mm (2 ft) heather with bright yellow leaves; and 'Robert Chapman', pale gold in spring, orange in summer and red in winter.

### COLOURED LEAVES

Gold, purple, silver or variegated leaved shrubs add interest for much of the year; evergreen kinds are specially useful in winter. All need an open sunny position or their rich hues will pale. They will thrive in ordinary soil fortified with manure and fertilizer

*The first chill October nights transform the smoke tree (Cotinus coggygria) from plain green to glowing orange, best seen against a dark green backcloth. Purple-leaved varieties are also available.*

## SHRUBS FOR FOLIAGE

| NAME | HEIGHT |
|---|---|
| **GOLDEN YELLOW** | |
| *Calluna vulgaris* 'Gold Feather' (heather, ling) | 230 mm (9 in) |
| *Erica cinerea* 'Golden Drop' (heath) | 230 mm (9 in) |
| *Lonicera nitida* 'Baggesen's Gold' (honeysuckle) | 1.5–2.1 m (5–7 ft) |
| *Philadelphus coronarius* 'Aureus' (mock orange) | 1.8–2.4 m (6–8 ft) |
| *Sambucus racemosa* 'Plumosa Aurea' (elder) | 1.8–2.7 m (6–9 ft) |

| NAME | HEIGHT |
|---|---|
| **REDDISH PURPLE** | |
| *Berberis thunbergii* 'Rose Glow' (barberry) | 1.2–1.8 m (4–6 ft) |
| *Cotinus coggygria* 'Rubrifolius' (smoke-tree) | 1.8–2.4 m (6–8 ft) |
| *Photinia* × *fraseri* 'Red Robin' | 1.2–1.8 m (4–6 ft) |
| **PURPLE** | |
| *Berberis thunbergii* 'Atropurpurea' | 1.2–1.8 m (4–6 ft) |
| *Corylus maxima* 'Purpurea' (hazel) | 1.8–2.4 m (6–8 ft) |
| *Weigela florida* 'Foliis Purpureis' | 1.8–2.4 m (6–8 ft) |

**Far left** *Richly scented mock orange* (Philadelphus) *has a particularly showy member in P. coronarius 'Aureus'.*

**Near left** *The leaves of* Photinia × fraseri *'Red Robin' open shining scarlet. Grown as a small tree or bush, it thrives in deep, rich soil sheltered from cold winds.*

| GREY/SILVER | |
|---|---|
| *Artemisia* 'Powis Castle' (lad's love) | 900 mm–1.2 m (3–4 ft) |
| *Buddleia fallowiana* | 1.8–2.7 m (6–9 ft) |
| *Buddleia* × 'Lochinch' | 1.8–2.7 m (6–9 ft) |
| *Calluna vulgaris* 'Silver Queen' (heather) | 200–300 mm (8–12 in) |
| *Cotoneaster lacteus* | 1.8–2.4 m (6–8 ft) |
| *Elaeagnus macrophylla* | 1.8–2.4 m (6–8 ft) |
| *Hebe pinguifolia* 'Pagei' | 150–200 mm (6–8 in) |
| *Hippophae rhamnoides* (sea buckthorn) | 1.8–2.7 m (6–9 ft) |
| *Lavandula angustifolia* | 300 mm–1.2 m (1–4 ft) |
| *Olearia* × *mollis* | 1.2–2.4 m (4–8 ft) |
| *Perovskia atriplicifolia* | 600–900 mm (2–3 ft) |
| *Potentilla arbuscula* 'Beesii' (cinquefoil) | 300–450 mm (1–1½ ft) |
| *Potentilla fruticosa* 'Mandschurica' | 1.2–1.5 m (4–5 ft) |
| *Santolina chamaecyparissus* (cotton lavender) | 600–750 mm (2–2½ ft) |
| *Senecio* × 'Sunshine' | 660–900 mm (2–3 ft) |

| VARIEGATED | |
|---|---|
| *Aucuba japonica* 'Crotonifolia' (spotted laurel) | 2.1–2.7 m (7–9 ft) |
| *Cornus alba* 'Elegantissima' (dogwood) | 1.5–2.1 m (5–7 ft) |
| *Elaeagnus pungens* 'Maculata' | 1.5–2.1 m (5–7 ft) |
| *Euonymus fortunei radicans* 'Variegatus' | 230–250 mm (9–10 in) |
| *Griselinia littoralis* 'Bantry Bay' | 2.1–3 m (7–10 ft) |
| *Ilex aquifolium* 'Golden Queen' (holly) | 3–4.5 m (12–15 ft) |
| *Kerria japonica* 'Variegata' (jew's mallow) | 1.5–2.1 m (5–7 ft) |
| *Pachysandra terminalis* 'Variegata' (Japanese spurge) | 150–230 mm (6–9 in) |
| *Ruta graveolens* 'Variegata' (rue) | 300–600 mm (1–2 ft) |
| *Viburnum tinus* 'Variegata' | 2–3 m (6½–10 ft) |
| *Weigela florida* 'Variegata' and 'Atropurpureum' | 1.8–2.4 m (6–8 ft) 1.8–2.4 m (6–8 ft) |

**Far left** *Non-flowering* Artemisia *'Powis Castle' develops a filigree of silvery leaves. Interplant it with yellow, blue, orange or red flowers.*

**Near left** *In autumn, winter and early spring, before much of the garden has awoken to the sun's warming rays,* Elaeagnus pungens *'Maculata' delights with its vivid show of gold-splashed evergreen leaves.*

**Red-berried elder** (Sambucus racemosa *'Plumosa Aurea'*) *Shrub. Flowers in April; fruits in July. Ordinary soil; variety prefers sheltered, partly shaded site. Height 1.8–3 m (6–10 ft). Root hardwood cuttings in autumn.*

**Scottish ling** (Calluna vulgaris *'Golden Feather'*) *Golden summer foliage turns reddish orange in winter. Poor, well-drained acid soil; exposed, sunny site. Height 300 mm (1 ft). Root cuttings of new growth in August.*

**Japanese maple** (Acer palmatum *'Dissectum Atropurpureum'*) *Slow-growing tree. Leaves purple in summer, crimson in autumn. Moist, well-drained soil; light shade, shelter. Height 2 m (6½ ft).*

***Elaeagnus* × *ebbingei* 'Gilt Edge'.** *Evergreen shrub. Gold-margined leaves; fragrant flowers in autumn. Well-drained, fertile soil; open, sunny site. Height 1.5 m (5 ft). Root cuttings in summer.*

**Spotted laurel** (Aucuba japonica *'Crotonifolia'*) *Evergreen shrub; male (non-berrying) form. Ordinary soil preferred; likes open, sunny site. Height 1.5–3 m (5–10 ft). Root cuttings in late summer.*

***Senecio* × 'Sunshine'** *Evergreen shrub. Leaves felted with grey-white hairs; yellow flowers in July–August. Free-draining soil; full sun. Height 900 mm–1.2 m (3–4 ft). Take cuttings in late summer.*

## ROSES
### BUSH ROSES
**Colourful, reliable, long-flowering and neat in growth, modern bush roses are especially suitable for smaller gardens. In flower June to October.**

| NAME | COLOUR | HEIGHT | NOTES |
|---|---|---|---|
| **Allgold** (cluster-flowered) | Yellow | 600 mm (2 ft) | Small double flower, slightly scented; glossy foliage; wide-branching growth |
| **Dearest** (cluster-flowered) | Salmon pink | 750 mm (2½ ft) | Fragrant, free-flowering; bushy growth; glossy, dark green foliage |
| **Iceberg** (cluster-flowered) | White | 1.8 m (6 ft) | Large, open flower; vigorous and leafy growth |
| **Lilli Marlene** (cluster-flowered) | Crimson red | 600 mm (2 ft) | Large semi-double flowers in clusters |

| NAME | COLOUR | HEIGHT | NOTES |
|---|---|---|---|
| **Josephine Bruce** (large-flowered) | Dark crimson | 900 mm (3 ft) | Fragrant, double, dark velvet flower |
| **Wendy Cussons** (large-flowered) | Rosy red | 900 mm (3 ft) | Fragrant; full flower; vigorous |

### OLD & MODERN SHRUB ROSES
**Old shrub roses demand space and are somewhat prone to disease, but include some of the loveliest roses of all. The modern shrub roses are more reliable with neater habit. Flowering season June–October.**

| NAME | COLOUR | HEIGHT | NOTES |
|---|---|---|---|
| **Cécile Brunner** (China) | Shell pink | 600 mm (2 ft) | Tiny shapely flowers, delicate form; free-flowering |
| **Fantin Latour** ('cabbage') | Pale pink | 1.8 m (6 ft) | Lovely double flower; free-flowering |
| **Frühlingsmorgen** (modern shrub) | Pink, gold | 1.8 m (6 ft) | Single open flowers, repeat flowering |

| NAME | COLOUR | HEIGHT | NOTES |
|---|---|---|---|
| Golden Wings (modern shrub) | Pale yellow | 1.8 m (6 ft) | Fragrant, single flower; graceful and spreading habit |
| Madam Hardy (damask) | White | 1.5 m (5 ft) | Perfect double flower, green centre; vigorous and leafy growth |
| Mme Pierre Oger (Bourbon) | Shell pink | 1.5 m (5 ft) | Cup-shaped double flower; neat, upright habit |
| Nevada (modern shrub) | Creamy white | 2 m (6½ ft) | Lovely open flower; wide-arching habit |
| Tuscany Superb (Gallica) | Crimson purple | 1.5 m (5 ft) | Double, deep velvet flowers; wide arching habit |
| Canary Bird (species) | Clear yellow | 2 m (6½ ft) | Single flowers; slender, arching branches |

## CLIMBING & RAMBLER ROSES

Climbers are best trained up walls, sheds, and pergolas. Ramblers, with more flexible stems are best for tumbling over structures.

| NAME | COLOUR | HEIGHT | NOTES |
|---|---|---|---|
| Albéric Barbier (rambler) | Creamy white | 7 m (23 ft) | Fragrant double flowers; dark foliage. Good screen |
| Albertine (rambler) | Copper pink | 7 m (23 ft) | Clusters of loose double flowers; very vigorous |
| Climbing Etoile de Hollande (climber) | Dark red | 6 m (20 ft) | Fragrant; will grow on north or east wall |
| Danse du Feu (perpetual climber) | Vivid red | 3 m (10 ft) | Large double flower; free-flowering |
| Gloire de Dijon (climber) | Buff yellow | 5 m (16½ ft) | Fragrant, free-flowering |
| Golden Showers (perpetual climber) | Golden yellow | 2.4 m (8 ft) | Short climber; flowers all summer |
| Mme Alfred Carrière (climber) | White | 5 m (16½ ft) | Small shapely flower; free-flowering, even on north wall |

## CLIMBING SHRUBS

All climbers need some vertical support. Self-clingers, like ivy and Virginia creeper, will adhere or hook themselves on to surfaces and do not need tying in. The rest need wires or trellis to guide and support the shoots.

| NAME, HEIGHT | FLOWERS | COLOUR | SITE | NOTES |
|---|---|---|---|---|
| Actinidia kolomikta to 4 m (13 ft) | June | White | Sun or part shade | Heart-shaped leaves, cream and pink. May be slow to establish |
| Campsis grandiflora (trumpet vine) 3 m (10 ft) | Aug | Orange scarlet | Sun | Not fully hardy: needs warm sheltered wall. Large trumpet flowers |
| Clematis 'Jackmanii Superba' 4–6 m (13–20 ft) | June–Sept | Deep purple | Sun or part shade | Prune as above |
| Clematis montana 'Elizabeth' 7–10 m (23–33 ft) | May–June | Soft pink | Sun or part shade | Prune in June only if necessary. Well-drained soil |
| Hedera helix 'Goldheart' (ivy) 2–3 m (6½–10 ft) | | | Shade | Self-clinging; small leaf with gold centre |
| Hydrangea petiolaris (climbing hydrangea) 2–3 m (6½–10 ft) | June–July | White | Shade | Self-clinging |
| Jasminum nudiflorum (winter jasmine) to 3 m (10 ft) | Nov–March | Yellow | Sun or part shade | Arching growth; needs tying to support |

**Above** *Heralding early summer with sumptuous single blooms, 'Nevada', a modern shrub rose, grows about 2 m (6 ft) high and wide and looks superb billowing over a sheltered patio or among the branches of an old, open tree.*

**Left** *Esteemed for its profusion of blooms on some of the longest, thorniest of climbing-rose stems, 'Albertine' enjoys three weeks of glory in late June and early July. Use it to camouflage an ugly garage wall, fence, or unshapely fruit tree.*

# TIMETABLES

In previous chapters we've had a look at the different types of location and soil required by garden plants, at ways in which to plan beds and borders in relation to the size and shape of different types of plants, and at the immense range of colours and textures available among annuals, biennials, perennials and shrubs. In this final chapter we consider all these matters in the context of time: how to organise work in the garden during the four seasons of the year.

## SPRING

### MARCH

Weather varies more in March than in any other month of the year. Gardeners in the North must take the time-lag due to the colder temperatures into account before sowing. In areas where the temperature falls below 6°C (43°F), plants, and even the turf, will wait to grow until April.

Meanwhile, the low rainfall and the drying winds result in good gardening weather, and there is no longer an excuse for delaying the digging. Make a point of skimming off the weeds first, burying them below ground as you go. Borders can be tidied up, stems cut down and the soil dressed with hoof and horn meal.

Rampant growers, in particular the aggressive Michaelmas daisy, rudbeckia, solidago, and saponaria, should be divided; replant young, healthy offsets.

Seedlings of half-hardy annuals (summer bedding plants) must be pricked out before they jostle each other, otherwise they will grow tall and spindly, and never fully recover. Hardening off should begin at an early stage.

Bulbs make an important impact on the garden scene this month. Winter-flowering crocuses flower in profusion and the blue, mauve, and purple cultivars of *Iris reticulata* come into full bloom, together with chionodoxas, *Scilla sibirica*, *Anemone blanda*, and the first daffodils (*Narcissus*). Later-flowering cultivars of the winter-flowering heaths (*Erica*) break into bloom, taking over from those that started in December and January.

Forsythias open their yellow bells, and the yellow Oregon grape (*Mahonia aquifolium*) and bright red and pink flowering quinces (*Chaenomeles*) begin blooming. Lungworts (*Pulmonaria*) produce flowers of red, pink, and blue, while the earliest leopard's bane (*Doronicum*) opens its first yellow daisies.

Finish putting in border plants and lifted trees and shrubs as soon as possible. Shear off the dead flower-heads from winter-flowering heaths that have finished blooming to keep them compact. Take cuttings of delphiniums and lupins as soon as the shoots are about 100 mm (4 in) high. Make sure each has a solid base, and set them in pots of rooting compost in a frame. Scatter general fertiliser around hardy border plants and roses and mix it into the soil surface.

Towards the end of the month prune climbing roses and hypericums; also deal with large-flowered (hybrid tea) and cluster-flowered (floribunda) roses and butterfly bush (*Buddleia davidii*) before the month is out. Layer shoots of deciduous shrubs to make new plants before their leaves get in your way. Plant a batch of gladioli for early flowers.

### APRIL

This is the month of hope and anticipation.

Warm sunshine is often followed by frost at night and if you are caught napping and a favourite plant is frozen, it should be thawed out by spraying with tepid water; afterwards cover it with bracken or paper.

As many nurseries as possible should be visited, especially those where ornamental cherries are in full bloom. The cherries are a great sight, from rather crude double-pink Kanzan of by-pass renown, to the more distinguished white gean, or wild cherry (*Prunus avium* 'Plena', also

*Scillas are among the most charming flowers of late winter. Best of its kind is* Scilla tubergeniana, *which produces three or more elegant 100 mm (4 in) flower spikes in February. It looks particularly good in association with snowdrops and winter aconites.*

known as 'Multiplex'), one of the loveliest of all.

Spring-bulb planting is the keen gardener's regular autumn chore, but comparatively few plant the summer-flowering bulbs in late March, and by not doing so miss a lot. In go Caen anemones, the single poppy flowers with black centres, and the richly coloured St Brigids, the galtonias or summer hyacinths, the exotic tigridias in exciting colours, and others that deserve to be seen more. Spring-flowering shrubs that have bloomed, and in particular the free-growing forsythia, can be pruned; and any last planting of rhododendrons or azaleas made towards the end of the month.

Daffodils and narcissi make a brave show this month, together with the early tulips, blue grape hyacinths (*Muscari*) and the majestic crown imperials (*Fritillaria*). Yellow leopard's bane flowers make a sunny display and are joined by *Omphalodes cappadocica*, epimedium, bergenias, and the earliest-flowering ajugas. Perennial yellow alyssum, purple to red aubrieta, and white arabis make masses of colour wherever grown as ground cover. The periwinkles (*Vinca*) start flowering in earnest this month, as do evergreen barberries (*Berberis*) and Jew's mallow (*Kerria japonica*), while the flowering crab-apples (*Malus*) and snowy mespilus (*Amelanchier*) cover themselves in blossom and the early-flowering brooms (*Cytisus*) burst into colour.

Sow seeds of hardy annuals to flower in summer. Also, sow seeds of perennial border plants, such as oriental poppies (*Papaver*) lupins, and coral flower (*Heuchera*) in a prepared seedbed out of doors if a lot of plants are needed cheaply. They are rarely up to the quality of named varieties, but help stock a new garden until better plants can be afforded. Plant gladioli for the main summer display. Start staking quick-growing border plants, such as delphiniums. Late April is a good time to put in evergreen trees and shrubs, including conifers.

## MAY

The weather can be very changeable in May. In general, north-westerly wind will dry the soil and a sudden drought may make watering of the newly planted a must. Meanwhile, late-May frosts sometimes pay us out for any foolhardy planting. Plants, too, can be caught napping, having responded to a mild spell and hot sunshine.

The battle against rose pests has now started. Combined insecticides and fungicides have lightened the work of spraying, but if the bushes are to be kept clean they must be sprayed every 10 days or so.

Get busy in the herbaceous border, staking, supporting, pinching any leggy growth, thinning out the Michaelmas daisy and delphinium

shoots, transplanting, weeding and sowing a few annuals to fill the gaps. Precautionary spraying against blackspot and mildew should begin in earnest. Delphiniums and other soft-stemmed plants must be defended against slugs, and the fast-growing seedlings of border plants encouraged with a dressing of fertilizer. All bedding plants and seedlings under glass should be given as much air as possible.

Late narcissi are joined by regiments of colourful tulips and the bluebell Endymion hispanicus. The pretty cultivars of the dead-nettle (*Lamium maculatum*) produce their pink spikes, which go well with the variegated leaves. By now all the plants grown for their foliage – silver artemisias and lamb's tongue (*Stachys lanata*), the hostas in wide array, the brilliant ajugas, the variegated and yellow- and purple-leaved shrubs – are contributing colour to the scene. Masses of blossom are provided by Japanese cherries, plums and almonds (*Prunus*), the flowering thorns (*Crataegus*), wisterias, and *Clematis montana*.

*The wild cherry (Prunus avium)* and *its handsome, double-flowered cultivar 'Plena' (seen here) are a lovely sight in April when blossom is at its best. The picture also shows how well the cherry associates with drifts of daffodils.*

# SUMMER
## JUNE

We seldom get a flaming June, but the sun will be at its strongest, and this is often the driest month. Watering becomes more demanding and those who have not been able to mulch the newly planted will have to work overtime with the hose once the sun has gone down.

Staking is essential: a sudden storm can play havoc in the border and ruin a year's endeavour. All herbaceous plants will be growing freely and will benefit from a feed of fertilizer or a drink of liquid manure. The gardener, anxious for first-class blooms, will have to pay attention to disbudding roses and border carnations. This entails keeping the large terminal buds and dismissing all smaller competitors. Now that summer has come, the pot-grown camellias and others previously kept indoors or in a greenhouse will enjoy a blow in the garden.

The rose-spraying programme that starts at the beginning of May must go steadily ahead fortnightly until the beginning of October. Blackspot can be treated with bupirimate and triforine, mildew with benomyl.

A whole host of hardy border plants, such as

pinks (*Dianthus*), delphiniums, lupins, peonies, day lilies (*Hemerocallis*), and oriental poppies (*Papaver orientale*) burst into flower this month, together with many of the hardy annuals sown earlier. New shrubs to flower include the early Dutch honeysuckle (*Lonicera*), potentillas, weigelas, hypericums, the climbing hydrangea, the potato-vine (*Solanum crispum*), jasmine nightshade (*Solanum jasminoides*), *Buddleia alternifoli*, and *B. globosa*. One of the glories of June, however, is the roses, which make a tremendous show of colour – even those planted the previous autumn and spring making a fine display.

Complete planting beds and borders with tender plants, including dahlias, cannas, and other bedding plants, as early as possible. Trim back brooms (*Cytisus*), aubrieta, and heaths (*Erica*) as they finish flowering to keep them bushy. Check upright conifers to ensure that they have not produced competing shoots at the top. Remove dead flowers as they fade from roses, annuals, and border plants as they fade.

## JULY

July does not always have the highest temperatures and the hottest days of the year. We can generally count on some very hot days in the South and South-West, but the fine weather may break up with a thunderstorm accompanied by rain or hail. Westerly winds may lead to July being one of the wettest months of the year.

Meanwhile, the flower garden should, in theory, be a riot of colour. Dead-heading must

be done daily, otherwise plants will lose interest in flowering and put all their energy into seeding. The tendency to seed is particularly evident in the short-lived annual.

Plants are still making rapid growth and will benefit from a feed of liquid fertilizer. Established roses will relish a pick-me-up after their first flush. Geraniums and other spring cuttings that are now well rooted should be moved on to 150 mm (6 in) pots before they become cramped and pot-bound.

The butterfly bush (*Buddleia davidii*) blooms, together with hypericums, the daisy bush (*Olearia* × *haastii*), Jerusalem sage (*Phlomis fruticosa*), the climbing *Schizofragma integrifolia*, many of the later-flowering, large clematis cultivars, and the dainty yellow *Clematis tangutica*. Extra colour is provided in borders by white *Chrysanthemum maximum*, the pink, daisy-like cone-flower (*Echinacea*), the blazing star (*Liatris*), and knotweeds (*Polygonum*). Border phlox also burst upon the scene, together with the brilliant purple *Salvia nemorosa*, dwarf dahlias, and all the summer bedding plants.

## AUGUST

This month's weather usually follows July's pattern. Atmospheric conditions are often similar and the two months add up to a fine or wet summer. Although autumn has not yet shown signs of taking over, plants and trees have lost their youth and many are becoming overgrown and blowsy. If rainfall is low, regular watering

will be called for, but the heavy dews will help to replace plant transpiration.

If you visit nurseries or garden centres, look out for the lovely Peruvian lily (*Alstroemeria ligtu*) hybrids in pink, coral, yellow and buff that flower through July and early August. Other plants worth tracking down are the beautiful, if not fully hardy 'Southern Belle' hibiscus from Japan and the fuchsias from America. Other plants worth finding are the dignified *Eremurus* or foxtail lily, the *Magnolia grandiflora* (the unique evergreen of the family), presenting its immense sweet-scented flowers just now, and the Californian poppy (*Romneya coulteri*) with grey-green foliage and petals of white, crinkled 'paper' that surround a golden centre.

Dainty Japanese anemones, golden rod (*Solidago*), ice plants (*sedum*) and tuberous dahlias take over the display in beds and borders as earlier plants pass out of bloom. Knotweeds (*Polygonum*) show their attributes now, and the charming dwarf *Cyclamen neapolitanum* adds to the display. It is also the month when the spectacular trumpet vine (*Campsis* × *tagliabuana* 'Mme Galen') opens its red trumpet flowers after a hot summer, and the bedding plants reach the peak of their display, as do some late cultivars and species of clematis.

Plant early-flowering bulbs, such as crocuses, fritillarias, chionodoxas, the dwarf bulbous irises, daffodils, and narcissi for a display next spring. Also set out autumn crocus (*Colchicum*) bulbs as soon as they arrive.

**Left** *Tree poppy* (Romneya coulteri), *a sub-shrubby perennial, opens its silk-petalled, fragrant blooms at the height of summer.*

*Butterfly bush* (Buddleia davidii *'White Profusion') attracts dozens of butterflies on sunny days in July and August. Other varieties have blue, purple, and bluish red flowers.*

**Above** *The false acacia* (Robinia pseudoacacia), *especially in its brilliant golden-leaved form 'Frisia', is one of the most elegant trees for the smaller garden. In mid-summer the foliage acquires greenish gold tints before falling with the first autumn frosts.*

**Above right** *An array of pinkish yellow berries follows white June flowers on the 'Aurea' variety of firethorn* (Pyracantha atalantioides). *Hardy and trouble-free, it is superb as a free-standing shrub, as a hedge, or planted against a wall.*

# AUTUMN
## SEPTEMBER

Michaelmas daises and Japanese anemones are still giving a lavish display, China asters do their best to hold attention, and the single daisy-like and button varieties have a certain charm; but annuals are almost played out, and the days are visibly shortening planting time is near.

If space does not allow for a tree, choose a large shrub. For those on acid soil it could be *Camellia × williamsii* 'Donation', a striking Himalayan rhododendron, or strawberry tree (*Arbutus*). More chalk-tolerant is the magnificent false acacia, *Robinia pseudoacacia* 'Frisia', with its elegant yellow-green foliage. The aromatic rosemary (*Rosmarinus officinalis*) is an accommodating plant that thrives in a light soil.

Other significant work this month is the potting up of 'prepared' bulbs in the home and greenhouse, the planting of daffodils, snowdrops and other early-flowering bulbs in the beds and borders (or in the grass if there is a wild garden), adding perhaps a few of the brilliant tulip species that do not require autumn lifting.

Many berrying trees and shrubs add extra colour at this time, including cotoneasters, pernettyas, cultivars of the mountain ash (*Sorbus*), and the firethorns (*Pyracantha*). Some of the first glowing autumn leaf colouring is provided by the snowy mespilus (*Amelanchier*). Many species

and cultivars of the dainty autumn-flowering crocuses and colchicums begin to bloom.

If peonies have to be moved or divided, this is the best time to do it; also the winter-flowering *Iris unguicularis*. From now until mid-October is the second period when lifted conifers and other evergreens can be moved safely. After planting, water them freely in dry weather. Prune rambler roses, removing or shortening the old stems and tying in the new ones to replace them. Many roses, especially ramblers, can be raised from cuttings taken now.

The tougher hardy annuals, such as calendulas, cornflowers (*Centaurea*), and godetia, can be sown now to provide larger plants and earlier flowers next season. Lift and pot any pelargoniums, tender fuchsias, and cannas you want to save before the first frost arrives; keep them in a warm greenhouse, or in a light place indoors, for the winter.

## OCTOBER

Flowers are scarce this month, but the berried trees and shrubs, alight with autumn colour, take their place. Here the mahogany paper-bark maple (*Acer griseum*), with dazzling red leaves, the orange fruits of the strawberry tree (*Arbutus unedo*), and the gorgeous flame of the sweet gum (*Liquidambar styraciflua*), play their part. If there is a trellis, archway, or wall where the magnificent Japanese crimson-glory vine (*Vitis coignetiae*) can ramble fancy-free, it will provide a blaze of exciting reds. This is a climber, quick and willing to camouflage any structure given a helping hand from the gardener. The lace-like Virginia creeper (*Parthenocissus quinquefolia*) and its forms give the same dramatic effect and have the advantage of being self-clinging.

Any gardener looking for an elegant addition to the small garden should consider Young's weeping birch (*Betula pendula* 'Youngii'), or even the decorative, common silver birch, known so aptly as queen of the woods.

The display of brilliant berries continues and the brightly coloured crab-apples (*Malus*) add to the show, some hanging on long after the leaves have fallen. Some autumn crocus and colchicum species continue to open their frail blooms, and many border plants, such as ice plants and Michaelmas daisies (*Aster*), hold their display well into the month, while others make a second, smaller, but nonetheless welcome showing. The first glistening pink blooms of *Nerine bowdenii* open now, as do the kaffir lilies (*Schizostylis*), and most bedding plants continue to be colourful until cut down by the first frost.

Complete the work of planting all bulbs (except tulips) as soon as possible. Weed any hardy annuals sown last month and thin them out to 75 mm (3 in) apart for the winter. Clear fallen leaves from low-growing plants. Lift and store gladiolus corms and dahlia tubers once their top growth has been frosted, or at the end of this month.

## NOVEMBER

This is the best month for planting hedges; here are a few of many: the dark and distinguished yew (*Taxus*) slow in growth; the beech (*Fagus sylvatica*) that keeps its russet leaves through winter (a copper beech planted here and there is a colourful addition); the holly (*Ilex*), often a slow starter, but with a useful prickly and resistant quality; the escallonia, a decorative seaside lover, but suitable for mild districts only; the easily pleased laurel (*Prunus*) or despised privet (*Ligustrum*), both willing and cheap (nine broad-leaved privets to one golden privet makes an attractive hedge). The hawthorn (*Crataegus*), tough and fast-growing, presents a fine boundary; *Berberis stenophylla* is decked with a mass of bright yellow flowers in April and May; rhododendrons also make a grand early-flowering summer hedge for the garden on acid soil; the sweet-briar (*Rosa rubiginosa*) forms a delightful scented fence from 1.5–2.5 m (5–8¼ ft) tall, while the cluster-flowered rose 'Queen Elizabeth' is excellent for the medium height informal planting.

As deciduous trees and shrubs shed their remaining leaves, the winter garden scene emerges, but provided it is well planted with evergreens it never looks empty and dead. The coloured-leaved conifers, especially, can provide plenty of variety. Also revealed when the leaves fall is the colourful bark of some trees and shrubs, like that of the coral-bark maple (*Acer palmatum* 'Senkaki'), and this is attractive the whole winter through.

*The slow-growing Japanese maple (Acer palmatum) has given rise to many cultivars giving superb autumn colour. This one is 'Atropurpureum', which grows to about 6 m (20 ft); others form smaller, bush-like trees (see drawing, page 54).*

# WINTER

### DECEMBER

There is no reason why December should be the bleak, flowerless month it is in many gardens. There is a number of winter-flowering plants that deserve room in any garden. The sculptured white blooms of the Christmas rose (*Helleborus niger*), sometimes tinted pink, and its interesting, hand-like leathery leaves make a wonderful winter show. The plant may be slow to settle down, but given semi-shade, a rich loamy soil that does not dry out, and a taste of manure in the spring, it will respond. The green corsicus (*H. argutifolius*), with clusters of dangling cups, the plum and purple *H. atrorubens*, and the Lenten rose (*H. orientalis*) hybrids are enchanting when seen nodding together.

**Below** *Best grown against a wall – even a north-facing one will do – Garrya elliptica delights with its slender silver-grey catkins (longer in the male form) in February and March. In the female form they are followed by clusters of purple fruits.*

**Above right** *The Algerian iris (I. unguicularis) performs best after a hot summer has baked its crown. Then, in October, it unfolds its beautiful flowers, which continue to open until late February.*

*Iris unguicularis* (syn. *I. stylosa*) from Algeria is another flower that no garden can afford to be without. Its foliage is untidy, but the lavender flowers that hide themselves in the tufts are beautiful. If picked in bud when they appear, resembling tightly rolled umbrellas, they will give a magic performance when brought into the warmth of a room. This iris should be planted at the base of a sunny wall where it can stay undisturbed; poor soil discourages flowering.

Another candidate for the winter garden is the climber, *Jasminum nudiflorum*, providing gay

yellow sprays during mild spells from autumn to spring. This is a willing grower needing rich soil, shelter, and regular tying in.

And, finally, give a thought to the winter heathers. *Erica carnea* (syn. *E. herbacea*), the mountain heath, is low-growing and excellent ground cover. Varieties such as rose-pink 'King George' are smothered in bloom from December to March. Other good ones include 'Springwood Pink' and 'Springwood White', of slightly trailing habit, suitable for furnishing a dull bank, while 'Celia M. Beale' is one of the earliest and largest of the whites for its size. *Erica × darleyensis* (one of the *E. carnea* hybrids) is seldom out of flower from November until the spring. Most ericas tolerate a moderately limy soil provided they are given a diet of damp peat and a place in the sun.

Among other winter-flowering shrubs are the winter cherries (*Prunus subhirtella* varieties), with their white and pink blossom, the golden-ribboned Chinese witch hazel (*Hamamelis mollis*) and the heavily scented maroon and yellow winter sweet (*Chimonanthus fragrans*). *Garrya elliptica* possesses intriguing green-grey catkins that arrive in February; they are particularly long and decorative in the male form. This shrub thrives on a north or east wall in a sheltered position. Finally, there is the shrub *Corylopsis spicata*, with fragrant, primrose flowers.

Take the opportunity of mild spells to prune leafless shrubs in need of attention. Also plant late-arriving shrubs and plants if the ground is not too wet and sticky: if it is, heel the plants in together in a well-drained spot until conditions improve. Tidy established borders, lightly forking over the soil among the plants. At the same time mix in old mulching material, and add a dressing of manure if available. Feed with bone meal established hedges and areas planted with bulbs. Border plants, such as Japanese anemones, perennial anchusas, and border phloxes, can be propagated from root cuttings taken now.

## JANUARY

This is usually the coldest month of the year. Conditions are frustrating for the gardener with many left-over jobs from December waiting to be done. If new plants arrive when the ground is frozen or very wet, heel them in temporarily in a 'warm' corner of the garden or put them in a frost-proof shed while the cold spell lasts; but they must be kept moist.

This is often thought of as a completely

colourless month in the garden, but there is quite a number of plants that bloom then. The winter-flowering jasmine (*Jasminum nudiflorum*) is generously spangled with bright yellow blooms that are continuously produced whenever the weather is mild, and some cultivars of winter-flowering heathers (*Erica*) are smothered in tiny blooms, shining even through the snow. In milder areas *Garrya elliptica* is hung with its long, silver catkins to give a charming display, snowdrops (*Galanthus*) have appeared in many gardens, and *Iris unguicularis* opens its lilac blooms throughout the winter months.

Towards the end of January, winter aconites (*Eranthis hyemalis*) begin to flower in the sunshine to provide a touch of sparkling yellow in sheltered spots. More colour is provided by the bark of some trees and shrubs, none more eye-catching than the brilliant crimson young shoots of the dogwood (*Cornus alba* 'Sibirica'), while the coloured-leaved evergreens, such as the variegated hollies (*Ilex*) and ivy (*Hedera*) and the golden conifers, create an impression of sunniness even on overcast days.

## FEBRUARY

Aconite (*Eranthis*), the winter-flowering 'buttercup', with an enchanting green collar, heralds the snowdrops, early this month.

Happily, the cold fails to deter the witch hazels (*Hamamelis*) or *Daphne mezereum* from opening their scented flowers now. The winter-flowering heathers continue to bloom profusely, regardless of frost and snow, while the winter-flowering jasmine and *Viburnum × bodnantense* open a fresh crop of flowers as soon as each cold spell passes. The first dainty blooms of the dwarf *Cyclamen orbiculatum* often appear this month and the yellow winter aconites (*Eranthis*) get into

their stride if it is sunny. The scented strings of pale yellow *Mahonia japonica* flowers open at the shoot tips, and the first winter crocuses open wide in any warming ray of sun. The dwarf yellow *Iris danfordiae* and blue *I. histrioides* 'Major' come into flower.

Retread the soil around newly planted trees and shrubs to firm it again when it dries out after heavy frost. Check posts, pales, trellis, and wires used as plant supports and replace or tighten any that are broken or loose before the plants break into new growth. The end of the month is the time to prune those cultivars of *Cornus alba* grown for the bright winter colouring of their young shoots, to encourage a new crop the following summer. This is the time, too, to prune all clematis plants except the small-flowered ones, such as *Clematis montana*, that bloom early.

**Left below** *Winter aconites* (Eranthis hyemalis) *are seldom seen en masse, but small clumps of them help to light up the garden in February and March.*

**Above** *One of the best winter-flowering shrubs,* Viburnum × bodnantense *has a powerful scent and bears clusters of pinkish white, tubular flowers in December to February. It grows to about 3 m (10 ft) in height and spread. Underplant it with smaller shrubs to hide its leggy lower regions.*

# INDEX

## Acknowledgements

The following photographs were taken specially for Octop Books: Michael Boys 13, 15, *19,* 25, *32,33,*36 right, 46 above, 49, 53 below right, 55 right, 57, 59 above, 60 left, 6 left; Jerry Harpur 6 above and below right, 8 right, 9 abov 11, *14, 17, 18,* (Cobblers) 20, 21 below, 22, 26, 36 right, 41, 42, 44, 46 below, 47, 50, 51, 58, 59 below, 60 right, 61, 63 right; George Wright 6 above and below left, 8 left, 9 belov 12, 16, 27, 28, 40, 48, 55 left, 62 right, 63 left.
The publishers thank the following for permission to use these photographs: Derek Gould 21 above, 31; Harry Smit Photographic Collection 52, 53 left and above right.
**Drawings** Bob Bampton 4–5; Sharon Beeden 22, 26, 30, 3 38, 39, 41, 43; Tony Hannaford 24, 29, 34, 39; Val Hill 7, 10; Nicki Kemball 44, 45, 47, 49, 54.